# Tales from the Dark Side of the Laundry Basket

By: Kate Van Gilder Hunt

I would like to dedicate this book to:

Jason, for giving me four reminders of him daily and for making me a better writer in his absence.

Oscar, Abraham, Nora, and Atticus, thank you for letting me raise you and for endless stories to tell.

Grief and loss…that's how this whole thing started. However, grief to me comes differently. Its meaning has changed to me over the years. As time moves forward, the grieving process does as well, but there are moments when it rings your doorbell like an unexpected guest. My husband and I lost a baby. We went in for our halfway point ultra sound, to find out our baby had died. I took that 'grief' and turned it into a lot of laundry, cleaning, baking, and realizing what I had, not what had been taken away before I even knew it. I started writing and I noticed, if I found the humor in what was around me…my kids, my life, my being out numbered in a house full of people who stand to urinate. The vast amount of silver linings that I had before me, it was healthier for me to try to focus on that than actual grief. Grief/loss to me is something very distinctive, it's like a fingerprint-no one does it the same. Writing is how I dealt with it then, and more so even now.

Little did I know at the time, the loss I started writing about was miniscule to what lay ahead…Losing my husband. He had always been my teammate, my best friend, my champion, my partner. It was sudden. It was painful. It was almost guerrilla like, nothing however really prepares you for it. I quickly realized that losing him would now change not only my life, but now the four children we had brought into the world together...I was going it alone.

I am a firm believer that there is no such thing as coincidence. The people you meet, the things that happen to you- they happen for reasons beyond your comprehension. Was my husband supposed to pass away, leaving me with our four children? Not sure about that one. However, during the time since his passing, it has made me realized my strengths and my weaknesses, and there are many. Having not gone through what I'm going through, I would never have known them. That, I feel, was his unwrapped gift to me. He continues to silently and invisibly help me from another rehlm. From this misfortune you rediscover the people brought into your life-past and present. They were brought into your life for a reason. They were placed there possibly long before you needed them. I feel lucky enough to have been given the gift to realize this.

At the end of the day, you write off your losses, hold onto your small victories, fend off the liquor cabinet, and try to find the humor in it all...the never ending journey of moving on. This is just the beginning of my story, Tales from the Dark Side of the Laundry Basket...

**Happy Meals are for chumps...Hi, my name is CHUMP.**

So, I'm one of THOSE parents not much longer...I dabble in treating my kids to fast food because, well, I'm lazy from time to time...and I justify it by thinking, "They'll play with that crappy 2cent toy for a while"- JUSTIFIED. Well, NO LONGER, it is 2011 after all, we are worth more than that? No, not really.

Remember a couple of years ago when there was that article that showed what happened to McDonald's French fries after sitting out for 3 months or something? Yeah, I wouldn't look at it. I wouldn't even entertain the notion of trying to get my brain around thinking that those French fries, while a completely guilty pleasure, were something that would/could gross me out if I thought about them. I DON'T WANT TO KNOW THE TRUTH? I'M WEAK after all...

SO, for lent we are giving up meat (fish only, except on Sundays- they really don't count) and (swallowing hard) fast food! Hoping I won't cave, I just need to plan ahead and not give LAZY a fighting chance...

On a lighter and true-to-this-household note, I am posting a picture of my future son-in-law, **Ernie**. I'm not sure if it was the **striped shirt** or the once tousled hair that attracted Nora to him? Who am I to question love? So there was an incident where Nora threw-up all over her man in her crib. Ernie had to be washed, and his hair was never really the same. **LOVE PUSHED THROUGH IT**.

Wondering how I would ever get Ernie away from her long enough to wash him again-and FUNKY wouldn't come close to what he was exuding. It was then that I realized we needed a DOPPLEGANGER soon, or we were going to be blamed for spreading the PLAGUE. Mission accomplished, found what could have been mistaken for the evil twin brother of Ernie. I handed it to Nora. She looked at it, and then at me as if to say, "…and who the hell is this?" Hoping to cleverly trick my 19 month old, if for just 4 hours so I could wash and dry this nasty little man-doll...Abe walks in and says (and I am writing this as Abe actually speaks-from dawn until dusk), "NORA! DID YOU GET A NEW ERNIE?! NORA, LOOK AT HIS NEW HAIR! IS THIS DIFFERENT?!"...thank you Abe for down-playing.

### ...so, there is Oscar...

So, 6 and a half years ago, Oscar came into the world. He was beyond a blessing, as we were told we would likely not get pregnant (I say we in this as a purely collective term-we know who did the work at the end) which is another long story for another day...

Anyway, Oscar is beyond a hoot! He has finally grown into his body, (don't get me started on the kids feet!) for a while there I thought we might have some Guinness Book kid on our hands...he did everything early, got teeth, later lost teeth at 4...walked, had

HUGE feet at birth, was wearing size 8 in pants when he was 5, write his name, draw...now it looks like I am bragging so I'd better quell this with a not so proud statement...He was a LATE talker. He understood what you were saying, and would answer in noises or sounds, but no words. Of course now he is OVERLY verbal as his teacher would attest to...but, I need to finish this thought. So, his first, full on word combination was when we were coming down the stairs from his nap and the neighbor's dog was barking (as it does day and night) and he said, "That stupid ass dog..." This, this was the first thing he said very plainly. It was then I realized, I'd better keep what I THOUGHT to myself. For a while everything was "Stupid ass", diapers, toys, juice. Thankfully, he grew out of it.

Last year he had a hard time with a kid in his class. I kept hearing about this kid who was kicking him, or hitting him at school. Even mothers of kids were telling me what they saw on the playground. When I finally figured out who the kid was, I was shocked-he was a shrimp! Oscar is the type of kid that will continue to take some punches before punching back. Well, about a month or so into school, I get **THE CALL**. The call from the Principal's office. The principal explained that perhaps Oscar had taken all that he could, and well, snapped...later to be known as "***The Scott Farkas Incident***". I pictured Oscar just losing it like "*Ralphie*" from *A Christmas Story*. Funny enough, the principal told me not to scold Oscar, the other kid had it coming, and probably wouldn't be bothering Oscar any more...

I've been thinking of all of this because his class did the mass yesterday at his school...he was the first reader. Now there is one thing you should know about Oscar; while at times he comes at you like a herd of elephants, he knows when to get gussied up... and for some reason he loves to wear a tie. He calls it "a handsome look". So I wasn't at all shocked that he would want to look like he was going for a job interview. He even had a chance to wear jeans, but he declined "it wouldn't be right" as he put it.

Color me shocked when I get to church to see, he is the only one who is dressed up! He looked sort of freakish next to all the rest of the kids, like a foreign exchange student on the first day of school (I speak of experience). Wondering if he had had second thoughts about his striped tie while everyone else looked, well, normal... Later, he just told me, "Too bad no one else had 'a handsome look' going, we were in the front of church after all..."

There are not a lot of words to describe Oscar- his name fits him. He doesn't judge anyone. He is, at times, naive but that is the beauty of Oscar. He looks one way, but isn't what he seems...and he loves to keep you guessing!

**...hi, my name is Abe, short for BUTTERS...**

I cannot be certain where the nickname BUTTERS came from-wait, I just remembered, and can you believe there is a story about it? Jason gave Abe the nickname of BUTTERS because, well for the lack of a better phrase, and I am quoting, "He was a pain in the ass..." For the first 6 months of Abe's life he wanted NOTHING to do with anybody, but me. He wouldn't eat, wouldn't sleep, and he just cried-except for me. I went to visit my dear friend April for 72 hours, he didn't eat the entire time I was gone. I remember my mom telling me when they would come by in the morning to relieve

Jason so he could go to work, he would just hand Abe to them and say, "Best of luck..." THANKFULLY, HE GREW OUT OF THAT...

There are so many things about Abe that are one of a kind. He is a comic, seriously, he tries to have timing, and usually it works. He regurgitates a lot of usually useless knowledge. Anything that wasn't directly said to him- a nice way to say "ear-hustler". Who am I to squelch the future ambitions of a CIA operative? I have often thought I might just try to talk to him while holding the phone to my ear, as that is usually when he hears every word I say. He is lovey but the next minute he is wild. The last 19 months he has been my right hand man- I was worried he'd feel replaced as the baby when Nora hit the scene...He just became the best non-paid "Manny" the world had ever seen. I really don't know how I am going to handle him going to school next year...who will I ask for fashion advice?

Now there are stories that are somewhat legendary around this house with Abe... Asking the creepy kid next door when his dad was going to jail...wearing a Santa hat the day after Thanksgiving through

Christmas...having a VERY limited internal volume. He is to the point where I can make the motion of turning down my imaginary hearing aid, and he does the same. The time he was wearing "...a little..." cologne that turned out to be toilet deodorizer. When it is warm out he would run around in his undies all day if you let him- and there are pictures to prove it! He loves to put on an apron "cook". Feels the need to bust a "fat move..." at a moment's notice, no matter where we might be-but especially in public, notably near breakables. HE IS "THE MAN, THE MYTH, AND SOME DAY LEGEND"...I can't wait to watch him grow up...and I'll be praying the rosary the whole time!!!!!

**...no need to open the Geritol, I'm just having my "dark day"...**

So, I knew it would happen, someday...I knew that I would have to deal with March 11th. I was cocky probably in the beginning, I held it together in a way that even inspired myself. I was "matter-of-fact" about what happened to me, knowing that I wasn't alone and I wasn't the first. My heart was heavy, but my attitude was "upbeat" (in quotes as I now wish I could channel it a little more). I dyed my hair, got it cut, did the laundry, went shopping, decorated for spring, made cookies, mastered my cookie recipe, spring cleaned, did Zumba, organized the basement, all within the last 2 weeks mind you, and nothing...Now that it is upon me, less than a week away, March 11th- I think I am going to require a "dark day"...

To begin with, I do not want anyone to think I am making a joke of losing a baby...I merely HAVE to use humor at times to realize that I am  only one person. One person of the millions who have, mainly silently, suffered. I seemed to find pride in the fact that I held it together in public. When people would ask me about it- and by the way if there isn't a polite way to ask about the loss of a child, chances are, it really isn't any of your business...but I digress. I wanted to hold it together, not just for myself but for my family. They didn't become less valuable to me after losing this baby. My God, without them, I wouldn't have known how blessed I already am.  Then there are friends, some of whom I was overwhelmed by their kindness, caring, and love. My family is blessed to have such people in our lives, and hopefully, you know who you are...

Here comes the part where I skip the co-pay, because you are possibly already too far in to turn back, and you get to be my therapist...by the way your office is way cooler than those on TV. After I lost the baby, still sounds weird saying "the baby". We still call him "YumYums" as we did when I was carrying him...wait that sounds weird like I set a place for him at the table. What I mean is when we pray for him at night. ANYWAY, at first I never thought about trying to get pregnant again. It was hard enough to go through what I did at the hospital. And when I say I, I really mean WE. My husband is a ROCK, and thankfully he is MY ROCK. It was such an emotional (even that doesn't describe it to the fullest) time, and through it there WE were. WE talked, cried, laughed when we were cried out. There are no words to describe how wonderful my husband is. I always knew that, like you can recite your weight for your driver's license...BUT it's like the only gift that *could* be gained out of this is knowing the strength of the love you have for each other. I guess that is the unwrapped gift that "YumYums" gave to us. When I think of it that way, I can smile through any tears that I may have.

**So, I feel the need to mention, that yes, I am having the "dark day" that I knew would come...Put the Geritol away, I got this...**

**...equal opportunity employer...**

...So I am wondering if I am giving my children the wrong impression. I'm wondering if they think I LIKE to do the following things. In my quest to not go all "NO WIRE HANGERS" on them, I wonder how I should attack the following problems that we have in this house. I realize these things are the "stuff that kids are made of..."category. And just because they are my offspring, I should overlook it...but THAT'S CRAP!! I feel it is my duty AS THEIR MOTHER not to send them off into the world thinking that these soon to be mentioned items are necessary for life function...

.....TOILET SEATS- you don't pee on them and if you do, wipe it up, and kindly put them back how you found them.

.....IF YOU HAVE TO GET NUDE TO POOP, PUT YOUR UNDERWEAR ON SITTING ON THE TOILET, if you have to sit on the floor to put your underwear on, make sure you don't leave any gifts behind for the next unsuspecting bathroom visitor- NO ONE WANTS THAT GIFT...

.....KLEENEX- can be RE-USED if only gently used to begin with, do not use 8 Kleenex to scratch your nose- and the trash can is the only place they need to be after that!

.....YOU DON'T WEAR YOUR PANTS INSIDE OUT, DON'T PUT THEM IN THE LAUNDRY THAT WAY- I think I sufficiently explained that one.

.....EAT OVER YOUR PLATE, USE a NAPKIN- can you tell how much I love to mop my kitchen?

.....QUIET DOWN- someday these kids need to work in a nursing home, if for no other reason they'll be around people who do not wince when they speak.

.....LEGOS, CRAYONS, STAR WARS figures, AND MATCH BOX CARS do not belong with you when you are pooping, eating, sleeping, or any other function needed for daily living.

.....WE CANNOT SAVE EVERYTHING YOU MAKE/CREATE/ INVENT- if you need to, rent a storage unit, our house is not big enough.

.....NO ONE IS DOING A LAS VEGAS LOUNGE ACT IN THIS HOUSE- thus, you do not need to change your clothes 5 times a day...

.....BRUSHING YOUR TEETH IS NOT "OPTIONAL CLEANSING" for the day...

.....I DO NOT KNOW WHAT I AM MAKING FOR A MEAL MORE THAN 2 HOURS BEFORE SAID MEAL-please do not inquire before you go to bed what we are having for breakfast- I have no fragging idea.

.....CALLING SOMEONE BUTT FACE ISN'T REALLY THAT FUNNY IN PUBLIC-no explanation needed.

.....**W*A*L*K!!!!!!!!!!!** -lost count of how many times in a day I say this...

...As Nora isn't able to attempt all of these said things, I am hoping to **break the cycle with her**, I am delusional I know....

**...are you there God, it's me, and I'm still folding laundry...**

So I have to admit, I remember reading the Judy Blume book *Are You There God, It's Me Margaret*, but all I remember about it is that it dealt with a girl coming of age. Maybe I didn't even read it, but I read the outside cover, thinking I would read it...? ANYWAY, when I think of this saying/line I think of those who I love dearly who keep me accountable to what I want in life, who I am, and why the hell I am still here in the first place...

My sister: I shared a room with her from birth, only later to share a bed with her until she went to college. Astonished she even speaks to me today. To list the disgusting things I had to outgrow- making it to the bathroom in time, snoring, talking in my sleep, and never giving her ANY privacy. She is the gal who laughs at all my jokes, taught me how to wear a bra, what kind of maxi pads to buy, and how to put on make-up. She was a tough act to follow, beauty queen, pianist, STRAIGHT A's, student body president, ETC. She is the one girl I was compared to the most when growing up, but she never made the comparisons, and for that I love her! She knows I am a total spaz and she loves me anyway! We took different paths to get to the same place and she is always there to hear me.

My mother: Sage with wisdom! Though she doesn't say much- does that make sense? She will hear out your problems, listen, and that's it unless she really thinks you need to hear what she has to say. But, sometimes that makes a world of difference, you know? We are different in some ways, but alike in so many others and those are what I am most grateful for. She gets me, and even when she doesn't she fakes it, and for that I am beyond thankful!

**I could go on about these two women, but I am not trying to recite an episode of the *Waltons*, so I'll stop....**

I am lucky enough to have a few "really great girlfriends", I write this in quotes as I sometimes feel I am so not worthy of them. I don't have to talk to them EVERYDAY, and sometimes we can go weeks, and talk and it is like no time has passed at all. These girls, I am lucky enough to call my "really great girlfriends", don't have to have everything in common with me, but they get me- a priceless commodity. These girls are those who sometimes I just need a "fix" of to keep body and soul together. These girls know the most about me, always make me laugh, understand who I am, AND STILL WANT to be my friend.

How could I be so lucky you ask? Maybe you are asking, maybe you are wondering why you are still reading this. I have no idea how I am so lucky to have these people in my life, but I can honestly tell you, without them my world would be a little sadder, more inebriated, and empty...Thank you, I hope you know who you are...

**...no, go and hide, I'll come find you...**

So when I grow up...(I say this in this way because then it gives me a goal/scape-goat not to already have these things I'm going to mention) I want a lock on my bed room door. I want to go to the bathroom and not have anyone walk in on me. I want to **not** be shocked to find Legos in my underwear drawer. I want to sit down for an entire meal without cleaning/pouring milk/or picking things off the floor. I want to not find tooth paste in places **no God fearing kid** would be brushing their teeth. I want to understand why it is so IMPORTANT to mention something to me BEFORE the sun is up.

...I want to not be asked a philosophical question before 8 am. I want to be able to answer said philosophical question before 8 am. I want to understand why one needs 5 Kleenex to blow their nose once...I want to sleep in. I want to make a meal that everyone eats without being prodded. I want to be able to leave the bathroom door open and not worry someone is using the toilet as a Holy Water dispenser. I want to put away toys and not find something I have been looking for, FOR WEEKS.

...I want to do a cartwheel-just thought I'd throw that one in. I want to know why boys flush the toilet BEFORE they pee and not after. I want to wear sexy underwear to bed and know that I will not have someone visiting me in the middle of the night to chat. I want to say something once and be heard. I want to not fold underwear-I could do this already but the OCD just keeps kicking in. I want to go on a vacation with the hubs...I want to stay up late and not dread the whole time I am up late how early I will have to be getting up.

...I want a family game night, where 5 minutes in you don't want to disown your family and move away. I want a cleaning lady. I want to look at a magazine and not be counting down the minutes I have till someone wakes from a nap, all the while listing the things I should be doing around my house during "free time"- which by the way is the biggest oxymoron KNOWN TO MAN around here...

......not too much to ask, you think? I'll get back to you on it...

## ...YOU CAN'T WEAR THAT, IT'S PACKED!!!!

So, do you want to know two words that bring terror to my otherwise happy-go-lucky life? ROAD TRIP. How caviler I used to be before I had children. I wouldn't even break a sweat on packing maybe "a" suitcase, the night before, hell even an hour before I got in the car. Sucker that I was, I never appreciated what I had when I had it. Now to be fair, every road trip we take to see my family and friends in Indiana gets easier as the kids age. But don't think I wouldn't do 15 cartwheels if we had an in car DVD player-we do not. I know some people who pop on a DVD in their car to run errands with their kids. My husband thinks they are wimps and regales in the fact that we are so hard core because we don't "need" such in our car, our kids "can handle it..." I don't know, I wonder how nice a 7 hour trip would be with one.........................................................sorry, I was dreaming a little there. I'M GETTING OFF TOPIC....

Yes, to get to my parents' house it takes us 7 hours, no matter how few stops we make, no matter what route we take, it's usually 7 hours. Now while this trip is fairly a breeze as we are not "potty training" anyone. Like the time I stopped on an off ramp to let one of the boys out to pee- even though we just left a McDonald's. He started to do the business, shadowed by the car, when I looked up and noticed that there was a house with a front window about 100 feet from us- GREETINGS FROM EXIT 45! Desperate times call for desperate measures! I have it down to a strict science now. The boys each pack a bag for the car- they pick the entertainment, I pick the snacks, a bottle of water, and a plastic bag. There is nothing like going 70 mph having 2 kids chucking up at the same time- literally been there done that. If they get bored, guess what, they packed the bag it's their problem. Nora is a tricky pickle though. Most of her fun is running from room to room picking up random objects, carrying on a conversation with/about them and then running to another room. Road trip to her equates to nightmare for me- but we make it work. Does anyone remember when they were a kid, going to sleep in their bed and waking up in the back of a station wagon/van and the family road trip started, all the while they were none-the-wiser? No car seats to adjust, no need to sit up, no need to NOT BE IN TOTAL COMFORT...the good old' days....

Before any of this madness starts I have to pack for myself and 3 kids. Jason "appreciates" when I help him pack, but just looks at me like, "You know, I've made it this far picking out my underwear, I think I can manage..." It's OCD, or habit, or me being in THE ZONE as it is called around here. Think about what ONE kid might use in a day-that's what I have to remember to pack!! It starts about 5 days out. Sleepless nights, laundry, laundry, laundry, checking the weather to pack the right stuff. **No, you can't wear that it's packed, if anyone tells you, 'You look like a SCRUD' tell them it's your mother's fault...I know those are your favorite undies, you can wear them at GRANDMAS!!!!!!!!**

It is for all practical purposes SELF INDUCED MADNESS, but having everyone content and settled while traveling is my life's ambition. Why the hell wasn't I a stewardess?!?! Have we ever came without the kids "lovies"? NO. Have we ever went without their meds? NO. Do they always have enough choices in clothes? YES. Did I remember to pack **my** underwear?! These are the maddening thoughts that will pass thru my head tonight and every night until we get on the road...

**...Really? Well, my 2 year old just cured cancer...**

So...we all know at least one. We meet them, we become sized up by them, and then, as it seems, we are **forever** annoyed by them...they are THE COMPETITIVE MOTHER=CM! (Insert scary music here: don, don donnnnnnn- sounds better than it reads)

As a mother, I am pretty apt to thinking that my kids are no better, no smarter, and no more gifted than anyone else's. They fart, pick their nose, and eat only cheese, and well they are typical kids. Don't get me wrong, when I started this journey called "motherhood" I was one of those saps who read books and tried to make sure that Oscar was hitting all the milestones at the right time. But then the strangest thing happened, he didn't do what the book said and I became scared that there was something wrong with him. Then I became **pissed at myself** for being sucked into some "benchmark" someone made for a kid they never even met. I swore those hideous, vial periodicals and books off THEN AND THERE. A kid will grow, and do what they need to do, and you can't do anything about it. As my children came into my life, I know

I am getting less and less stringent about anything that they do. Don't get me wrong I give a "WHOOP WHOOP" when it is due, that is one of the many gifts of being a mom. But the devil is in the details. Don't fret and it will all work out in the end. In saying this I also know that I can be a "momma bear" when I need to. I feel a healthy balance of a "Mother Bear" from the Bernstein Bears and Beth Chapman(from Dog the Bounty Hunter) get me where I need to go in life-minus Mrs. Chapman's boobs, I don't know how she gets anywhere with those...I'm getting off topic.

So there is this mom. I've known her for a few years, and with every child she has and every child I have the competition for her has been on. Don't get me wrong, at first it sort of put me off, but then it just became humorous. Every action that my child made, for what I thought was normal, typical, and frankly not illegal, she would notice, comment, and somehow one-up me. But the fantastic ending of the story doesn't nearly end there....

So this last fall, my parents are in town and wanting to eat at Maid Rite (my dad had never been there and now never needs to go back, he says) for lunch. We walk in, and there is the competitive mom=CM at the next table. We say hello, somewhere from the hello she manages to one up me, and then lunch continues. Now I have to say, when it comes to eating out, my kids ROCK! As long as there is food in front of them, they do a great job and can blend into even the fanciest restaurants. So we are sitting there, chatting with my parents, and my mom (who noticed the one-up-hello) says, "What the devil is wrong with her, her kids are acting crazy? She's not alone, she has two other adults with her..." I love my mom, and I noticed the same thing, but my mom sometimes thinks "her whisper" is actually quiet (I LOVE YOU MOM, BUT YOU NEED TO KNOW THE TRUTH-don't cut me out of the will). The competitive mom finishes lunch and comes over to the table to say goodbye. She says to me, "How do you get Nora to sit in the highchair like that?" I said, "Well, she just does, she doesn't really have a choice..." and smiled, noting that her kids were everywhere but sitting all during lunch.

A couple of hours later, my mom and I are having coffee and I mention the CM (competitive mom) and how crazy she is. My mom said something, probably not realizing that it would stick with me

**forever**…every time I feel like I am at my wits end, when I feel like the crappiest mom ever. My mom said, "Kate, did you not realize what happened back there? You didn't try to make an excuse, you just said 'Nora doesn't have a choice, she just sits there...' YOU ARE A GREAT MOM, and your kids are proof of it just by looking at them..."

So now I am to the point when I THANK the CM (competitive mom). Every time she has to mention what her kid has done, be it writing novels, dusting/sweeping the house, curing cancer, talking in full sentences at 9 months...Every time some ridiculous "one-up" comes out of her mouth, I hear my mom...over our coffee chat, and I have to smile. Thank you mom, I needed that...

**...Opie, are we in Mayberry YET?**

I am going to be brutally honest....I detest technology! Don't get me wrong, I love the fact that I can vent my innermost-crazy-ass-thoughts and someone may or may not read them. I love the fact that I can keep in contact with friends and family at a touch of a button. I love the fact that even when I am at my most bored (rarely happens) I can read up on something I never would have before. The technology that I can do without is that which I call "kiddie technology". **I know I am BEYOND BACKWARD** but I do have a point in this fledgling rant...

Kids. You have them. They grow. Suddenly they want things that cost more money than you have spent on yourself outside of your mortgage. Kids, much like adults, see what others have and of course are intrigued, they want to know more, they want to have "that sort of fun"....my question is, what the hell ever happened to just good 'old fashioned playing OR learning from something that was not plugged in? Why must fun include no human interaction, no thought processes, AND cost $180?

I realize that technology surpasses you at a rate unthinkable. I realize that my kids will be able to do on a computer at the age of 9 what I was doing when I was 19. I realize that stunting them of any of this makes me a bad mother. But then again, what's so wrong with wanting your kids to be KIDS. Naive, creative, exploring a world that is new and exciting, learning from the same things that I learned from- the outdoors, books, newspapers, and GLAMOUR MAGAZINE? I figure I am 35, and I have earned the right to be more or less than tech savvy, my kids have the rest of their life to be smarter than me... when they are adults.

**I live in a dream world**. Look at my "profession"-an idyllic house wife and mother of 3, keeping the home fires burning. Everyone has clean underwear, everyone is clean behind the ears, sack lunches, school snacks, the house is somewhat presentable, cocktails are chilled by 4, and dinner is on the table by 5. If you didn't know any better, you'd think it was 1957. **I WAS MEANT TO HAVE THE PROFESSION THAT I DO**, and I am happy with it! But, in that dream world, my kids want the same things I do. Living a simple but very happy life. Finding the joys in things that have NOTHING to do with technology, gaming systems, MP3s, or live chats. I know, dream the big dream Kate... Opie, I don't think we are in Mayberry yet...and I am pretty sure I'm talking to myself, Opie is on his I-PAD...

**Like sands thru the hourglass, no seriously, these are the days of my life....**

First off, I don't like the night-life, and I don't like to boogie. Just pondering life. Sundays are one of the best days of the week around here, pretty much for everyone. We have a pretty good breakfast. Head to church (getting ready for church is the only STRESS involved in the day). Make "Sunday Dinner" and dessert (usually enough food to feed 20-but left overs are what it's all about). Finally, a "quiet night" for me. Jason head's over to a buddies house and they 'play x-box' but I know they are painting their nails and talking about girls. ANY WHO Sunday night, after a pretty nice day, is my time to clear/clean my head out, fold some last minute laundry-it never ends-maybe paint my nails and watch crappy 'girlie' TV, usually something on Bravo. But, tonight I am trying to remember where my week went...

Drove back from Indiana on Monday-we are never driving through the day again! My kids can get pretty excited by a somewhat mundane adventure, and night driving is it. Yeah, sooner or later they fall asleep. My kids always have a great time in Indiana, and it is the best "stay-cation"! We get spoiled by my parents, get to see friends, and cocktail time rocks- my mom makes the best appetizers, why bother with dinner?

Took Nora and Oscar to the doctors this week. It's like they need to start a support group for those two. As if I never ask him how he is feeling, Oscar treats going to the doctor's office like a lounge act. He knows when to hit them with a joke, go for the hard press on what ails him. And then always wants to know if he needs to take his clothes off? Does he need to lay down? (Buh-duh-duh-ching!) *'Thank you ladies and gentlemen, please remember to tip your wait staff, you've been a great audience, Good Night*!'

Now Nora on the other hand...you think someone was walking her into an institution and telling her "we'll pick you up next week..." She cries, she seizes, she whimpers, she throws her fists to the air. This is all before we even see our little 4'9" tall Filipino doctor, who calls her "Norrdda" and calls me "Momma". THEN THE BIZ STARTS! It amazes me that the doctor can even know what the hell is wrong with her she is such a spaz!

Got to go out with the hubs this week. Had a great dinner, chit-chat, and sort of felt like adults w/o kids for an evening, VERY RARE! It was so nice, it was almost like I saw it on a movie and it didn't really happen, good times.

Abe has decided that we are getting his shots this week. He has already figured out what he is going to order from the ice cream shop afterward-it's good to have goals. He also has figured that being a know-it-all is still pretty fun. He likes to now remind me of what I am doing as I am doing it, as if it wasn't going on unless he mentioned it. Nora and I were watching TV upstairs Saturday night. Abe came in the room and he walked out of the room backward with his hands up sort of in front of him, and said quietly, "I'll leave you two alone..." It is things like that, that will either get him in trouble next year, or married off- not sure which.

The saddest news in our house this week, is that the Queen died. Long may she wave from her balcony up in the sky...? It only took 24 hours to get the low-down of who broke her, but I am leaving her out as a reminder. Do NOT CLIMB ON THE TOILET TO TOUCH THE SOLAR

POWERED WAVING QUEEN, she isn't yours, you are just lucky enough to pee in her presence....RIP.

**Attention all ladies...the candy man is OFF the prowl...**

So I know it is a staggering double standard...boys are different than girls. Even though this has no validity, as a parent, I feel like it is inevitable. The boys probably will be able/get away with more than their sister. As a girl with a brother, this was something that infuriated me. Especially when I knew that I wasn't doing or even attempting to do HALF of what my brother did growing up. BUT as a parent you do your best and frankly hope for the best, and that is all you can do...I'm getting off the point.

So, among Abe's preschool classmates, there seems to be a vast number of girls to boys. It was the same with Oscar's class, but he declared after the first day who he wanted to marry, so man of mystery he was not. With Abe, he kept it pretty secret. Don't get me wrong, I'm not trying to marry off my kids at the age of 5, but it is interesting to know their "type". Let me further clarify, that when Nora is 5 and naming off who her boyfriend is, I will be changing the subject so fast heads will spin-**there's the rub**- THE DOUBLE STANDARD! But, I'll cross that <u>rope bridge</u> when I get to it.

Back to Abe...It is a topic of discussion about girls in the house because there are more of them than boys. Also, because Abe is as tall as a couple of girls in his class-fairly tall. My untrained eye would assume that these would be the girls he'd be "into" because they were roughly the same size. Usually he dismisses the entire topic, knowing that he can't be faded on his personal life. Yesterday, while waiting for our cell phones, he decided to spill his deepest, darkest secret- WHO HE HAD A CRUSH ON. He opens the conversation by saying, "I have a secret, and it is about who I like in my class"...

"Really, Abe...do tell..." I said. To which he let me know in no uncertain terms that if I wanted to know his deepest darkest secrets, as if he were in the KGB, I'd have to pay for them....in sugarless gum. I figured it was a pretty fair trade, discussed the negotiations, and an agreement was made. "I like

Isabelle..." he said with a rather large grin on his face and the reddest cheeks ever seen.

Later on I asked him why he liked this girl (she is very cute, and follows him around a bit)? His answer was short, intelligent, and very to-the-point, "...because she likes me". Okay, seems fair enough. It was only the next morning when he was explaining to Oscar the 3 reason's he liked Isabelle that had me worried...

....#1. She is nice.

....#2. She is cool.

....#3. She is foxy.

It was too early to respond to a conversation that I was only listening in on. _Note to self_: start drinking coffee earlier in the morning! So it seems, while Abe has the biggest blue eyes you've ever seen, currently they are only for Isabelle, because she's *so foxy*....

**...things mothers of one should not say aloud...**

Anyway, I am with these mothers today and I am watching them multi-task like NOBODIES business, still they are holding down conversations the whole time. Impressive. They opened up about their everyday things, and it was nice to feel like they aren't trying to be SUPERMOMS they are just doing what they do. Very impressive. Then the topic turned...and this is where it gets interesting...

Let me be the first to admit, I willingly have my children. I am not enslaved by anyone to procreate, then subsequently have to rear these children against my will. I understand that for whatever reason you have children, the quotient of children is YOUR PERSONAL CHOICE. Here is where the topic gets juicy...

....if you were talking to someone who was a leg amputee, would you ask them if they'd been jogging lately?

....if you were talking to blind man, would you ask them if they'd seen last night's sunset?

....if you were with a deaf person, would you ask them to listen to your favorite song?

**No you wouldn't...because whether you
know it or not, it is sort of rude
and discourteous to do such a thing....**

So, this being said, if you have one child, I
am very happy for your choice. Children
only make your lives worth living. However,
if you only have one child, please be
mindful that you have AN ABUNDANCE
OF TIME ON YOUR HANDS! If you don't
believe me, I have a few phone numbers of
moms that I think you need to look in on and
realize that multi-tasking can be, and it
should be revered as an **art form!**

**...here comes Peter Cotton Tale...**

So many fantastic childhood memories
surround Easter...besides the everyday egg
hunt. My family growing up made holidays
special. No matter what we did. The fact that
we usually never went anywhere as we lived
in my father's business, a funeral home.
While living in a funeral home is a WHOLE
other blog...

Easter. Growing up Catholic, Easter was THE BIG CELEBRATION….After spending the 3 days before in church, rather solemn couple of days at that. My mom tells of the story that my brother once asked her on Good Friday in church "who's the guy on the cross..." and "if he went to Bremen's?" the other funeral home in the town we lived in. BUT we are talking about THE CELEBRATION...

My MOM worked her TAIL OFF!! Food was always something that was planned out ahead of time. Usually it was something festive and fun, never the same every Easter. The whole holiday, from a special breakfast (hot cross buns!!) to dinner and my mom always made some of our Easter candy; marshmallow, chocolate eggs and suckers, coconut nests etc. No, no, I don't have a lot to live up to...We'd basket up the ingredients for our Easter dinner and take them to church to have them blessed when I was really little. We went to a little Polish church that had such traditions that I remember to this day. But, food was always good, made from scratch, and the labor that went into it. I probably didn't appreciate it then, as a mother I do now! All the little things that I remember, I know they were because of her.

We always colored Easter eggs in the
SAME CERAMIC CUPS EVERY YEAR.
Always trying to be more creative than last.
This tradition still holds on and my sister
dyes eggs all year round she loves it so!
These eggs were never hidden, we always
hunted the colorful plastic ones with an
assortment of candy and pennies in
them...but it wasn't your average hunt...

My dad went wild for the egg hunt. He hid
them in one part of the yard- *as if he were
hiding them for navy seal training*. They
were everywhere, on the roof, in the gutters,
up IN trees. As if that weren't enough, as if
the thrill of that wasn't enough for us, there
was THE SILVER EGG! A pantyhose egg
(wow, dated myself!) stuffed with lotto
tickets, a $2 bill and the good stuff! But one
year the hunt went a-rye. My dad had to stay
home to answer the business phone(again,
what did we do before cell phones) and on
the way home from church one Easter
Sunday we were radioed in our station
wagon to "TAKE THE LONG WAY
HOME, I REPEAT TAKE THE LONG
WAY HOME". Hard, considering we lived
two blocks away. It seemed my dad's handy
work with the eggs intrigued one of the
neighborhood kids (you know, the kid who
is always around, always at the back door

when you open it) he had taken the "challenge" and started hunting.

And so, it's almost here, EASTER! And while I am looking forward to ending Lent, I have 11 days to get a ton done. To try to make Easter as special as I remember it, and to start a couple of crazy traditions of our own. BRING ON THE MADNESS!

## ...hoping that ticking isn't a bomb...

So, I'm not sure if I have run out of laundry, turning a blind eye to the house cleaning, or if I just need a project 24 hours a day. Lately I have been inundated with strange reminders. Like strange occurrences, you know the ones that "come in threes" or something...

A few weeks ago I was under the impression that I should get out a copy of the Book of Mormon that I have. It seemed everywhere I went I was bumping into smiling Mormons. The culmination of this week is when I saw a young Mormon missionary wipe out on his bike in front of my house! I thought this was quite a cosmic nudge from the other side. But, Joseph Smith came and went...

This week I have been inundated with reminders of babies. Maybe it is the laundry/storage Goddesses (I'm sure they exist) telling me to go thru Nora's things, or maybe it is my biological clock keeping me up at night. As if I want madness/chaos at all times to keep me on an even keel? I randomly, in the last few weeks, have thought I was pregnant, just because I have felt tired, listless and have had that surge of PSYCHOTIC HORMONES that I tend to get when with child. Either that or I have a yet-to-be-diagnosed case of mono, who knows. I feel like I should be happy with what I have. But, there is this "pang" to have more of what I have. Does any of this make sense? I'm 35 years old, I don't have forever. I don't want to "know" much freedom (going anywhere without carrying a duffel bag of baby necessities) until I am done procreating. I have come up with various projects to try to get my mind off of this "pang", but it doesn't seem to be working out. Of course I could always clean my house...Nah.

I heard Abe call Oscar a "dummy" the other day, Oscar scoffed it off, but then I heard

Abe say, "wow, that felt good..." As if getting that out is all he needed to move on with his life. Ah, to be five again, but he might have been onto something. Today I heard a news story about how they have done a study finding out that swearing, at times, can be good for you! It releases endorphins and regulates your body's need to level itself out during stressful situations. So if you stub your toe, you are allowed by your body to say, "Shit" and get on with your day.

So it seems I will go busy myself with a well-deserved project, hopefully something necessary. OR, if you see me out, walking in the store or something, randomly spouting out profanity, do not be alarmed. I am regulating the biological ticking in my body. And by all means, feel free to act like you don't know me...

**...so I figure maybe Jesus and I could hang...**

Well, I've been at this for two months now and I feel like it helps quiet the voices in my head. I realized they have actual medication for that, but I wanted to explore my options first. Seems like when I get these random thoughts out of my head, they're gone. No, I mean really gone. Like I hardly remember what I wrote afterwards. Maybe I need a different medication for that? I sit here, kids and hubs already in bed from a long day. And there, not 7 feet away from me, is a hamper of laundry. A teeming hamper of laundry. I figure we have undies and clothes for the morning, and it can pretty much sit there. Seven feet away from me, leering, and I'll get to it tomorrow...I call that progress.

So today, in church, I had a strange list going on in my head. I listened to the homily, funny and insightful, and then my brain sort of shorted out. Probably because Nora fell asleep on me and both of my arms were asleep. So I figured if I could get my mind on something else? Not the right direction, but I digress... (The following is based on stereotypical theories from me and well, society...here goes)

I started thinking of all of the things Jesus, you know the son of God and I had in common. Now on paper, you'd say NOTHING. But my mind trudged on...

-First off, we have pretty similar hair. I mean, I've never seen the guy with a bad hair day. But I really feel a kindred spirit to anyone with a wave in their hair. It's tough to keep that stuff under control!

-Next, he had followers...I can totally understand that! Ask me. Ask me the last time I have done anything without someone following, right behind me mind you, anywhere? The pantry, the bathroom, you name it, someone is following me. That is unless I ask them to, and BOOM another similarity.

-A sandals and a caftan. I love them. I would wear them all year round if it might not gross people out. Well and if the later were even considered a dress "do". But the sandals? I am all in-leather, plastic, smelly, I'd wear them.

-He loved his mother, and why wouldn't you? They brought you into this world. Even if yours might be a train wreck, you have to be thankful to them for creating Y*O*U!

-He knew what it was like to clean up after a house full of men. Not all mine are men yet, but it's no picnic.

-He's the go to guy for advice! Anything you need to know, I'm pretty sure he'd have the answer. Like a walking GOOGLE. Who would go behind his back and say, "That Jesus, what does he know?" Ah, hello? EVERYTHING, he's freaking Jesus! Seems like the kind of guy who'd have your back.

-Lastly, who wouldn't want to hang with someone that could turn things into food and wine? Ah, hello? I'm pretty sure he was on every guest list after that shin-dig in Cana. I too like to be prepared for what "might be" at a party. Okay, this is hardly a comparison, but still a pretty good reason to hang with the guy.

THE DIFFERENCES...

-Okay, so he wanted everyone to know his name. Not me. I'd rather you forget my name. Some days I get so tired of hearing "Mom...Mom...Momma...Mommy. MOOMMM!!" I finally just announce, "Mom has gone. My new name is Felicia"(not sure where this name came from, but it cracks me up to hear Abe say it, maybe that's why). And my kids really do it. Just this afternoon Abe said, "Felicia, can I have a snack?" I told him," Felicia was on her 10, and maybe after that." I have used the alias, "Regina Phalange" when necessary...

-The HEAT. I live in Illinois and I can't stand the end of July. How in the world could the guy even think straight in all that heat?

It seems to me that the similarities outweigh the differences. Who wouldn't want to hang with Jesus? So, as I start another month of random ramblings, I'm curious where my left brain will take me. I apologize, that was just 3 minutes of your life that you'll never get back.

## ....might not have it all together...

What's that saying? "We might not have it all together, but together, we have it all..." That has been playing thru my head the last few days. Not sure if it's the fact that Abe is officially a kindergartener (we have the paperwork to prove it), having a friend with a very sick child, or the end of the school year ahead. Summer is literally within spitting distance, and I have to say I'm looking forward to it.

I "grumble" a lot about what I do day to day. I am mentally grounded enough to know that I am one in a million who do the same things. Only I am lucky enough to stay at home with my kids (a-hem, HUBS, this is a shout out to you), and for that I am GRATEFUL. At times socially cut off from other adults, but ECSTATIC that I get to be so active in my kids' lives. Is it tight at times financially? Sure, but I figured on buying my Bentley and getting the boob job after the kids graduate from High School. Anyone who knows me should laugh at this.

I try to start putting things into perspective this time of year. Remembering that next year at this time all the "hum-drum" things that are creeping up like bad underwear will be gone. All **new** "hum-drum" things will be on the agenda. Time flies too fast. I asked Abe what his summer job was going to be now that he was a graduate. He just sort of looked at me funny, and said, "I think I need to learn how to read and drive first..." Way to keep it simple Abe.

I'm looking forward to "attempting" to piggy-back structure with fun this summer...yeah, I just sort of chuckled when I read that back to myself. But, I've got a goal, and here it is...

## **Summer 2011**

~try to have fun every day.

~worry less about laundry, more about engaging with my kids and teaching them something. Wait, maybe they could learn to DO THE LAUNDRY!

~try to keep some structure in the "day to day" around here. When that goes missing, the liquor cabinet seems to want to be opened.

~get outdoors!!

~work on spending indoor time with the TV OFF.

~catch fire-flies.

~see a few Quincy Gems Games.

~DATE NIGHT, DATE NIGHT, DATE NIGHT!

So, as yours truly, starts to mentally attack her summer vacation, please take note:

*While we might not have it all together, together we might have it all...*

### ...so, these kids are going to keep growing, I guess.

In the interest of full disclosure, I am 3 feet from a teeming laundry basket...it'll be there later, right?

Well, I am now a mother of a second grader, a kindergartner, and a full on "almost 2 yr. old" drama queen. I felt it coming on yesterday. MOODY...was an understatement. I realized after a cocktail and responding to a few threads on Facebook (NEVER- I repeat, NEVER a good idea). I am a little overcome with the notion that my boys are growing so fast... It seems as if it were yesterday that they were going to the library for the first time, or still needing to hold my hand walking across a parking lot. I'm lucky to get more than a grunt good-bye in the morning. Although the other day, I ACTUALLY got a kiss from Oscar…only to be asked if I was wearing lipstick? Yeah, I was still in my pajamas.

It seems when I was in full on mode with the boys (two under 19 months), I DREAMED of the day when I would have a few hours to myself. Consecutively. Now the notion of only having Nora under toe next year almost frightens me. What the devil? I am naive to think to myself, who will I talk to all day without Abe here? Then recanting that thought, knowing by August Nora will be talking my ear off and telling me if my skirt is too short, my hair is messed up, or what I was wearing looked like pajamas.

I am vigilant this summer to take the time to make mental notes about these offspring I call my children. So often these kids crack me up, and because I need a stronger dose of GINKO BILOBA, it is forgotten. Now don't get me wrong. I'm not going to make a point all summer long to GUSH how quick witted my kids are. Mainly mental notes.

Abe….the other day at the Museum here a lady asked him to sign the guest book (I don't think the lady wanted us to leave-we might have been the only ones in that day). I told her that he was just "starting

Kindergarten", but Abe agreed. He made the first letter, and she gushed. He made the second letter, and she oohed and wowed. He started writing the third letter, looked up at her and said, "Now wait for it here it comes....here comes the exciting part..." I almost peed my pants...

Oscar...I just heard him tell Abe, "you can do what you want, but if you want me to play with you, you are going to have to quit acting like a SPAZ...the choice is yours..." I'll take that over his first words "Stupid Ass Dog" any day...

Nora...couldn't contain herself at the school picnic today while the music was playing. She was hopping around here and there, and whenever anyone came up to her to try to dance with her, she WAS NOT HAVING IT...then she discovered the pool cue and things started to look like they might get a little violent. At one point she was lying on the dance floor with my future son-in-law ERNIE.

The fact remains, these kids aren't going to slow down, so I'd better step it up and remember all I can before I have a diagnosed issue for it!

**...so, it's summer...**

I think I am missing a gene. I am in a major minority in this house and what seems like the world. I DISLIKE SUMMER. I can hear the gasps of terror brought on by what I just said. Sadly, I own this, and my kids, no matter how fun I try to make it, totally know it.

I am the 'one' who sees some stores putting up fall displays and internally "frolics" at the notion. I become giddy when I see school supplies. I begin to smile when I see the stores trying to start selling sweaters in July. I AM WEIRD.

I could blame this of a variety of things. It doesn't help that on all of the 'summer holidays' my husband (even if it is his day off) has to work, not indoors, but outside grilling free food for customers at his store. THIS YEAR THEY HAVE ADDED THE 4TH OF JULY to their line up with a hot dog eating contest! When these days are winding down, I am so exhausted of my kids asking "what do we do now?" or "when is dad coming home?" By 5 pm, when the party should get started, I am spent! Again, I AM WEIRD.

The only salvation to my psyche during the summer is that there are two birthdays to celebrate! Strange as it seems, my kids only have parties on 'even' years, this saves on my sanity and my wallet! I have less than a month until I make a LEGO birthday cake for Oscar (bless his little 7 year old heart for picking something easy). It looks to be something fun, and possibly easy to make! I'm looking forward to it!

Nora on the other hand...wants NOTHING GIRLIE!! I keep showing her doll cakes, or Hello Kitty cakes or butterfly cakes. Not having it! Her repeated response is, "Ernie cake...I yike Ernie cake!"...I'm going to keep lobbying for something else until the very end!

What is the inevitable point to this tirade? While you are at your 4th of July party or Labor Day party, I will be at home making a list of all the things I will be doing when summer is over! Happy freaking summer!!

## ...so, dun, dun dunnn...we're still procreating!!!!!

So it seems, when you become pregnant with your first child, it's as if there are parades held in your honor. Midget circuses visit your town and you glide around sort of feeling like, 'you are the only one this has ever happened to...' Then you become pregnant again. People are hopeful and excited for you to have a growing family, well wishing you on to a new adventure. By the third time you are pregnant? All of this wanes. People are happy (though you secretly know they are trying to figure in their head how in the world you will manage it all) and congratulate you. Any announcement of pregnancy after that, people might as well look at you and say what they are thinking…YOU PEOPLE ARE STILL PROCREATING!!?!?!  HOW MANY ARE YOU GOING TO HAVE?!?!?!...end scene.

So, I have started this about, well, about a BILLION times since June 14th, 2011 in my head. At 10:30 at night, in my parents' bathroom, there I was, staring at a pregnancy test...a little unsure of what I thought about what the test was telling me. POSITIVE. Really? I mean, really? Then I do the math in my head. Yeah, really. So, in my parent's quiet house, at 10:30 pm, I call my husband sort of wishing that I was telling him in person instead of over the phone. My husband IS SEETHING WITH EXCITEMENT…as any man should, knowing the accomplishment of creating another human being.

Jason is a BABY MAN, loves them, cuddles them, and has a strange ZEN QUALITY for them that I am seriously MISSING. He completely knows what to do immediately to calm them and soothe them.  I, do not enjoy babies (I know, I am missing a gene). I like a "baby" pretty much when they can tell me off, OR start laughing, and not at their own gas. So, Jason is SO the Yin to my Yang. Without him (for obvious and various reasons), I wouldn't be able to even enjoy those first few months of a new baby.

So, here is something you'd think I would try to figure out. I usually find out I am pregnant when it seems like I am 2 or 3 days along (honestly, more like 5 weeks but I am hormonal-go with it). Thus, my pregnancies seem like they last YEARS, we are talking elephant gestation. So, in an effort to try to keep my sanity, my psyche, and my hormonal outbursts to a low...I am waiting to post this until my first doctor's visit at 10 or 11 weeks...I am slightly gun shy at getting TOO CRAZY about this after having lost a baby. I am hopeful, thoughtful and prayerful (not sure it's a word) that all will go well this time around. And ready for THE ADVENTURE!

**...so, Yeti's have feelings too...**

So, we ARE back to school...Tomorrow is the first "official" week of school. Why must they start things up mid to end of the week? Give the kids a taste of 'structure' and then, WHOO HOO IT'S THE WEEKEND?!?!?! Hormonal tirades aside, I did however learn a few things this week...

My boys are obsessed. I am not really aware of who to blame. The boys are taken over with **BIG FOOT FEVER** (insert dramatic gasp then pause here). I said ***BIG FOOT FEVER*** (as my voice has sort of an echoing quality about it). AND NO- we are not talking about a Yeti. Full on SASQUATCH. Yeah, I don't get it either. I have no real exact idea where they came up with this notion. Do I blame *Animal Planet* for having "Finding Big Foot" on this summer? Do I blame the movie *Judy Moody and the Not So Bummer Summer*? I want to believe that their fascination, their quest for the truth lies in one movie, ***Harry and the Henderson's***. Thank you Jason and Netflix. They have scoured my back yard. Sprayed bug spray on anything that will stand still (there is a long drawn out reason, but really, semantics). They have "claimed" with fierce determination, that they have seen something lurking by our garage. So, I'm pretty much ready for school to start, FOR REAL...

So, the REAL bit...I find it interesting to know what sort of first impressions my kids get from things. Truth-be-told, they are usually right. They are young enough with little filter, but smart enough to see the truth. Abe has a teacher that is revered in this house hold, seriously, you say her name and I swear you can hear <u>a choir gently singing</u>. He, just in the orientation, picked up a couple of her quick witted bits of humor. She's like an old girlfriend, not a lot of mystery...but still a lot of fun.

Oscar has a 'new to him' teacher who we are really excited about, she seems to understand how to get through to kids his age...Yet, we are also saddened and praying for her daily as she has cancer for the second time, and will have to undergo more chemotherapy this school year. I really feel blessed (and please take this the right way) that he has someone who can possibly, without even trying, show him a vast amount of strength, courage, and faith. He was quick to point out that he liked the way she had a reward system, and "sometimes you get BONUS bunny bucks without even knowing it...by doing something nice just because..." REALLY, ON THE FIRST DAY YOU CONVEYED THAT MUCH? Freaking awesome is all I have to say...

Nora, she spent the week blissfully unaware of what is about to happen. On the first day of dropping Oscar off she said as we were pulling away, "I lost my Oscar..." Multiply that by about 236,000 when Abe is gone all day..."*Life __without__ your brothers gets hectic...*" Soon enough we will fit into a rhythm of some early morning shopping, possibly a coffee/chocolate milk date. **We** have until February, and then we are going to be a bit hermit-like for a while. As long as we have DVR-ed her favorite shows, all is right with her world...

According to my estimations, I will be getting LOADS done while the boys are in their educational institutions...I am talking a staggering amount of laundry, house cleaning, dinners, phone calls, and catching up on all those re-runs I have already seen of *Gilmore Girls*. I am figuring this is all fairly monumental, the very first free time of its kind in 7 years- I'LL TAKE IT...even if it is only a 2 hour span...

**...Helen Reddy has nothing on this girl...**

So, it would appear to the naked eye that I am some house wife. Trapped in her own existence, seething to do something else ONCE THE KIDS GROW UP...but that just isn't the case...

First of all, it shouldn't go without saying, I AM LUCKY! I am lucky to be able to stay at home with my kids. I am lucky that I do not have to get dressed in anything more than pajamas to get my job done. I am lucky that my husband understands how important it is for our family that I stay home, and I understand that not every woman has/wants this luxury. We aren't bathing in $100 bills at my house, but we (my husband and I) make it work because it is important.

Now, don't let all that deceive you into believing that I am some sort of door mat, who knows not much more than the schedules of the *Disney Channel,* the best price on laundry detergent, and 58 ways to hide vegetables in a meal. I have VIEWS on what is going on in our country and city for that matter. Anyone who wants to discuss it, BRING IT. I know enough to not open with such things in common discussion at the grocery check-out. Women, and especially house wives, shaped popular marketing not more than 50 years ago. We were the ones that were targeted in ad campaigns, we were the ones companies wanted to gain trust with, and no amount of posturing was unnoticed. I think many women today forget that, I have not. When I first became a stay-at-home mom, my life was riddled with misconceptions. Sure I can do what I am doing in my pajamas-BUT STUFF HAS TO GET DONE AROUND HERE, or I'm not doing **my job**. I just do it listening to a wide variety of things: talk radio, NPR, and PBS for kids. It's pretty interesting when your 4 year old knows what time it is because, "**LUSH RIMBAUGH**" is on...

While my day to day does not compare to that of many other women I know in the work force. I find that it is the differences in us that make us unique. So, why has this come to light? Why must Helen Reddy take the fall? Well, first of all Helen was Australian, she wouldn't really know the burdens of American women, would she? And it comes to light now, as I feel not everyone is being heard in this country. And seemingly, if you are "heard" you are an extremist. I'M HERE TO SAY I AM NONE OF THOSE THINGS, or Canadian for that matter...

**...so Fantasy Football is neither FANTASY nor FOOTBALL ~ discuss...**

I try to stay on top of things in this world. I know a smattering of current events, keep up on the Kardashians, although I know very little. Ask me something about any show on the Bravo Channel? I KNOW WAY TOO

MUCH! I know enough about most topics that I can hold a conversation with pretty much anybody. This brings me to football ~ I've got nothing.

This has been an on-going crisis in my house hold for more than 10 years. The hubs LOVES HIM SOME FOOTBALL. So much so that he can't even be bothered to cheer for one team. He has played fantasy football for so long that there really IS NO OTHER WAY OF LIFE. I love that he loves football, and I see it (in my head) as so much fun to watch football and get excited by the minute to minute action. But the big game comes on, and NOTHIN'. I have studied, asked questions, and TRIED MISERABLY to "get into football" but I just CAN'T.

For a few years when we were first married I called myself a 'football widow' and the tradeoff was he'd watch it somewhere "fun"- 'cause let's face it, that wasn't here. I'd get some sort of payoff at the end of the season. I believe at one point it was furniture (and no, I'm not that spoiled, we have a bit of a connection). The payoff ended when we had Abe. I guess we weren't in need of it as our house became filled with toys instead of furniture.

THE POINT OF THIS STORY? I swear I am getting to it...

I have tried everything. I will watch you longingly and maybe be jealous of you. I am ready to admit defeat. I don't understand it. I can't get excited by it. I will never have any yearning to watch it.  "Hi, my name is Kate...and I am MISSING THE FOOTBALL GENE..." Happy football season to all the rest of you!

**...THE PREGNANT RANT...you've been warned.**

So, this was bound to happen. I am up at any given hour of the night, hopelessly trying to will myself back to sleep. Not wanting to get out of bed to go to the bathroom (for the umpteenth time). Thinking...SO, here it is, and if it makes any sense, you may want to contact your local metal health physician.

My kids are growing. This of course should come as no surprise, it is eventually going to happen. BUT, the rate at which my kids are growing is mind boggling. Between contemplating how often to buy pants in one year for my boys. Seeing them become "boys" and not 'my little boys' is really chapping my hide. They have all this personality, and then they go to school and get someone else's personality. It all gives me reasons to cherish every irritating antic that they pull. Lastly, wondering if there may be 'hand-me-downs' that I cannot for the life of me find, because I have no collective memory anymore. 'They're growing boys...' Yes. I know this. I am just terrified at the rate of which they are growing. Makes me THANKFUL I am not Amish...

Then there is the case of the two year old girl who finds it necessary to narrate her entire day, and in between times mine. Yet when we are in public, she is practically MUTE?! Not to mention the fact that she has learned a few words that OF COURSE she doesn't say in her otherwise cute 'dutchie' way, but PLAIN AS DAY. Example: While driving down 12th street the other day to take the boys to school she lets me know that "she does not have a PENIS..." Seriously? Seriously. I don't even know what age I first said that word? I don't even use proper terms around here! I shudder to know what she is talking about at the age of 10.

Then we have world events. Yep, at 2 a.m. I'm plagued with thinking about what is going on in this world we live in. Tonight, for example, I know I will be wondering about Muammar Gaddafi. I noticed today watching the news something that I do not understand. The news was talking about Muammar Gaddafi's latest video released. Then suddenly I look at the bottom of his video, and there is a "sign language bubble". He is ranting on and on, and there is a fella in a "sign language bubble" signing like there is no tomorrow. This got me wondering. WHY? Why is there a 'released' video from this numskull, who just whines about the same old thing over and over, and THERE IS ANOTHER HUMAN BEING IN A SIGNING BUBBLE, and that is necessary? Are there that many of his followers who are hearing impaired? Just wondering.

...and Jason, my dear, if you are reading this, yes, you have heard this rant already...thanks for listening.

**...etiquette for getting hit by a school bus...**

So, a school bus hit my mini-van (Lord, how I wish they were called something else, something cooler...like fascination mobile?). No damage. No injuries. Nothing to complain about, except that "technically" the whole thing was a "hit and run". That right there is what gets me about my whole morning. Here comes what I hope is a politically correct rant.

So, after I called the school systems bus "hot-line" and was told the dribble I had presumed I would hear. "The driver did not know that she hit you, so she kept moving..." Really? What's done is done, but anyone who knows me in my current condition knows better.

I put on one of Nora's favorite shows and got in the shower. While I was lathering up, I really started to get LATHERED UP! Thinking about what/how the whole accident happened this morning. Was I speeding (I tend to do that-though not in school zones)? No. Was I fidgeting with something in the car not to notice the bus?

No. Was the bus stopped at the sign or still moving as I was passing it? Not sure. Once the bus hit us (really, more like nudged us- but it could be felt by my kids) I stopped. I noticed that the bus stopped also. I got out of the car and THAT'S when the bus started pulling away. So, by definition, I'd call that a hit and run.

Of course, hair not done, still in p.j.s, not wearing a bra, looking sort of like a crazy bag lady. I put the car in reverse and followed the bus. When I caught up to the driver she said, "Are you okay, I didn't see you. Thank goodness I didn't hit you!" WHAT? UM, MY TWO BOYS IN THE BACK SEAT (feeling like they are on an episode of COPS) WOULD DISAGREE!

So, that's my story. I am grateful I drive my kids to school every day. I'm grateful no one was hurt. My kids and my "SWEET PICKLES" mini-van (still not cool) are still all in working order. I guess this is just a public service announcement. I am fully aware when I "curb" my mini-van, but a Quincy Public School Bus Drivers are not fully aware when they hit something...

**...so, I'm not going to let 'Kris Kringle'
bite me in the...**

It's that time of year again...wait a minute,
it's actually another homogenized holiday
season. I'll admit, I let 'Fall/Halloween'
creep in this house a little too early. By
October 27th I was pretty much over it...sad,
as 'Fall/Halloween' is one of my most
favorite times of year. Bygones be bygones,
it's done and I'm sickened to even look at
Halloween clearance...I've moved on, but I
am going to keep my control and not let Kris
Cringle bite me in the ass as the last holiday
season did.

I have urges. I'm woman enough to admit
that. BUT, I am ~~wanting~~ yearning to not let
any opportunity get past me that I can learn
something/teach my kids about greater
humanity. ***Charlie Brown Thanksgiving***
best describes what I am getting at. Why do
you need anything more in life than a
Charlie Brown Holiday movie? Seriously.

**Marcie**: *Don't feel bad, Chuck. Peppermint
Patty didn't mean all those things she said.
Actually, she really likes you.*

**Charlie Brown**: *I don't feel bad for myself, I just feel bad because I've ruined everyone's Thanksgiving.*

**Marcie**: *But Thanksgiving is more than eating, Chuck. You heard what Linus was saying out there. Those early Pilgrims were thankful for what had happened to them, and we should be thankful, too. We should just be thankful for being together. I think that's what they mean by 'Thanksgiving,' Charlie Brown.*

I don't want the holidays to come and go (especially one with the word THANKS right in it) and not try to express to my kids the idea of gratitude and thankfulness. The feeling of 'receiving' is alright, **but the feeling of 'giving' is so much better**.

So, today we started the ritual of "giving". Going thru all that they had and "giving" things up that they no longer played with, wanted, or needed. Sadly, I think only one of my kids understands this whole transaction, but one out of 3 isn't bad. We might do it in stages, I think all at once was a little unsettling for one of them. He started going around the house, like Steve Martin in **"The Jerk"**. He'd pick up random items, talking to them as if it were understanding that he "saved" them from extinction. While it was humorous, it saddened me that he couldn't see the forest for the trees.

AND don't even get me started on what they are "wanting" for Christmas! The hubs and I decided last year LESS IS MORE. We feel like our kids have ALREADY taken over our house, why add more to that every December 25th? "Jesus was given 3 gifts, so that is all my kids get"- I stole that from a mom a couple of years ago and thought...GENIUS!!! ...there is a double lesson there, love it! So, that is how it rolls in this household. In reality, it makes our kids REALLY think about what they want for Christmas and that it shouldn't be about the quantity rather the quality.

So, on this 5th of November, while I read of friends on Facebook playing Christmas music and watching Christmas movies on the Hallmark Channel, I am willfully resisting the urge until at least November 25th, and then ALL BETS ARE OFF!!! Until then, enjoy all that this time of year has to offer you!

**...and there she goes again...**

LET ME JUST START THIS WHOLE THING OUT WITH THIS SIMPLE BUT UNDER-RATED STATEMENT: ***MY HUSBAND IS A GOD***!!!! He has put up with 'prego-me' for the last 34 weeks and I don't even think I could have done that.

So it seems that I have traded in possibly the VERY BEST thing about being pregnant…nesting. There is no rhyme or reason for WHY in the world you NEED/WANT/DESIRE/OBSESS about cleaning. The fact-of-the-matter-is you do, and it is possibly the one time of my life I can see my refection in the shelves in my refrigerator...

It seems I have traded the beloved 'nesting' with crying-jags and isolationism I'm about one flannel shirt from being Ted Kaczynski. The mood swings? The rate of which happen too often, in horrible places, and well, at all. If I don't answer the phone, it might just be for your own good, you know? I'm not talking about watching a Hallmark commercial and crying about that, I'm talking just looking at my kids (usually after a said mood swing) and seeing their beautiful face covered in Nutella or wearing

sunglasses or being creative and
I...JUST...LOSE...IT.

Currently, whilst seeing my doctor I have
mentioned such things. But appearing in her
office with nothing short of a unicorn horn,
she gives the same answers to all the
questions/concerns I have, "...well, every
pregnancy is different..." With a head tilt
and a smile...'cause that makes CRAZY
okay.

I feel as though I should have this under
control. I've done this all before. I have
OCD and I'm willing to admit it. Then I
think of my 7, 6 and 2 year old...Where did
the time go? Was I this BAT-CRAZY with
all of them? To which the hubs would
lovingly say, _yes_.

So, this is my challenge. My quest for not
letting the next 6 weeks go by and not
appreciate my beyond wonderful
husband...my verbally obsessed, loud,
typically wonderful boys...and my tiny diva,
who is also overly verbal, bossy at times,
and loves to give hugs...

**...so, hello old friend...**

To think how long it has been since I last put
fingers to keyboard to silence the voices that
speak at me day AND night. Then again,
I've been a little busy bringing a new male
into the world, Atticus. While he mainly
eats, sleeps, cries, poops and EATS, he
definitely sets the day to day schedule. It
puts my OCD into hyper drive (the whole
'not an infant person' doesn't help either).
BUT, I figure we have 4 or so more months
to get to know each other and then we'll see
if we'll be friends. Because really, that is
what it is all about if you think of it...

This strange nurse handed me my new born
son, and a thought crossed my mind...okay,
so, now what? If this were an adult that you
met for the first time, you wouldn't just grab
them, start cooing to them, and proclaim
your love. You'd tell your other friends,
"Yeah, I met Atticus, seemed like a pretty
chill guy, don't really know much about him,
but he didn't tell any lewd jokes, so yeah, I'd
talk to him again..." I guess that is just how
my process works. I'm into personalities. So,
I have about 4 more months to check out
this kid, size him up, and see what he is all
about. Every morning about 2 am, it's sort of
like I'm talking to a bald guy that I don't

know really well, but I know that it'll build every day.

Now, since bringing our latest home, my other kids have seemed to grow up over night! Oscar and Abe have been dabbling at becoming more independent, policing themselves, and climbing the cabinets on a daily basis to 'make breakfast'. Nora, well, she has just become known to me as *THE REGULATOR*. Seriously, no one should feel sorry she is the only girl, it's her brothers that should be pitied! And it has been eye opening to see of my kids, who still needs some snuggles more than others now and then. I guess I'm surprised because it isn't who I expected. They have all become 'experts' of sorts in the various ways of helping with the baby. There's 'shushing-duty', 'pacifier-duty', 'throw-away-duty', and lastly, 'would-you-hand-me-that-duty'. To which *THE REGULATOR* informed me that if I said, "please, thank-you, and you're welcome, it would all happen faster..." BURN!!!!

And then there have been the set-backs that I have had in the last 3 weeks that have not only made me grateful for the ability to walk without pain, but also for my Mother-in-Law, who has been able to swoop in and help out in a moment's notice. There aren't enough 'thank you' for that as I am CHRONICALLY BAD AT ASKING FOR HELP! I'm sure there is a clinical term, but it has escaped me at the moment.

But, as always, the blessing of having a baby is that it is also made ABUNDANTLY CLEAR that I couldn't do any of the above without my husband. He is my best friend. He picks me up when I need it the most (even did a little shopping for me-shoes and a dress!). I love him dearly, and I am counting the days until we can have a "date-night" and wear my new shoes!

**...so, my mantra is mind over matter...**

The word **incapacitated** might come close to describe me in the last 3 weeks. Two months ago I was blissfully 'worried' about how I would handle four kids, the balance of an infant in my already busy life. Little did I know what I was in store for...?

So, I woke up about two weeks after having my 4th baby, and noticed that my leg sort of hurt. I shrugged it off and kept on going. By 8 o'clock that night not only was I not able to walk, but brought to tears due to the pain. Sleeping, sitting, walking- all painful to the point where my left leg just became' DEAD', literally having to pick it up to move it. I then spent the next 2 weeks seeing a chiropractor due to a pinched nerve only to admit to myself that I was not getting better. I was in pain every minute of the day. No medications or adjustments were helping. As if it wasn't frustrating enough to have an infant, the simple fact that my pain management was UNMANAGEABLE. It's affected my family, and my ability to function mind, body and spirit.

You know it's bad as you hobble into the doctor's office and some 80 year old man, you don't even know, comments on the fact that "...wow, it's tough going, huh?" So, after seeing my doctor, I was told by my insurance that I would have to wait over a week to get any tests done. I HIT THE WALL. Waiting over a week, with this pain? I ended up in the ER, due to the fact that I needed SOME ANSWERS as to what the exact name of the HELL I'm living is. Turns out I have Lumbosacral Radiculopathy...fancy name, huh? Well, folks, it's pinched nerves...awesome. Physical therapy is the next step in the road to recovery. While I wanted a quick fix, you can't always get what you want.

The trip to the ER brought me to the realization that the last 3 weeks, my life has SUCKED. Sadly anyone around me, yeah, their life has SUCKED just as much! It was then I decided that I HAD to flip the switch. I had to develop the mantra, "this is mind over matter" and really, that was the only option. And along the way, I have a new found respect for my husband, family, and friends who have been able to swoop in, help out and most importantly, make me laugh when I want to cry.

As I hobble along hoping to start some sort of physical therapy within the week, I am constantly reminding myself that when this CRAP is all done (let's face it MONTHS from now) my life will be so easy and wonderful all at the same time. I'll be able to sleep in the same bed as my husband. Take my kids to the park. Make dinner for my family. Go on a date. Basically, just function...something so simple that I took for granted.

*This is when life as I knew it changed. It is at this point that my blog sort of became less me again ranting of being a mother and a wife. From this point on, it's about dealing with LIFE. As a widow, grieving. A mother of four, coping through a new life. While finding the humor in my life helped me heal, it also became my silver lining. When times became more than I thought I could handle, somehow humor would find its way through. I feel it necessary to add this. I feel like we always had funny stories to share. Then life changed without notice. While humor would keep me from eyeing the liquor cabinet before happy hour, we had to work harder to find the humor from this point on...at times we did, at times we didn't, but this is how I dealt with it.*

**...two weeks ago...**

Two weeks ago. Two weeks ago I was buying my husband's birthday gifts, knowing I'd give most of them to him that night, I can't stand a surprise. Two weeks ago tonight I went on a dinner date with my husband cutting it short so we could go home and put the kids to bed. Two weeks ago my life was hectic, tiresome and for what I thought, normal. And then it wasn't.

Two weeks ago I was frazzled about having a party here, scurrying around to make sure that everything was clean, fancy and fabulous...what I would give to 're-do' two weeks ago.

Two weeks ago I knew that my husband loved me, and that despite that love we hardly EVER took the time for US. Two weeks ago I never thought to watch him sleep, intently listen to his voice, remember the best way to hug him, look at my hand holding his, spoon him, or even to remember his laugh...

The next thing I know I am throwing on clothes, some that weren't even mine (I think I wore one of the boys stocking caps to cover my bed head) and driving 80+ miles an hour down highway 61 to try to get to the emergency room. The whole way pleading with God to somehow not take this man from my life.

Twelve hours later I was standing looking at my sobbing refection in a window, still pleading with God to somehow spare him. Actually trying to bargain with God, that if he could just get Jason through, we would pay it forward some way. Praying. Praying. Praying, somehow he would be the strong willed person I loved and he would rally. Wondering how I would tell my children if anything ever happened to him? How would I survive?

I stared at him, holding his hand, his arm, anything I could get my hand on, not knowing what to say. What do you say to someone who has loved you? I don't mean love, I mean LOVED you. How would I tell him how much he meant to me, would he ever actually know? Then reality.

Letting go of someone you love. I pray that no one reading this ever has to do it. Sadly, some already know what this is like. It is a pain. It is a pain like nothing else in the world. It aches and tares at you so intently that you think for that moment you may just stop breathing...but you love the person that much, you know there is no other way.

I laid my head on his chest and whispered to him. The words at that moment just seemed to roll out of my mouth, almost unconsciously... I thanked him.

I thanked him for loving me. I thanked him for being the love of my life. I thanked him for my beautiful children. I thanked him.

Now life as I now know it, keeps rolling on. Meals to make, bills to pay, laundry to do, children to nurture and hopefully remind them of their father every chance I get. Thankfully for me, I remember two weeks ago tonight.

**...'there'...**

I have to be honest, I didn't know much about Canton Missouri before I moved here. I liked the fact that we were close enough to a Catholic Church and the kid's school (they ride their bikes! love it!), that we could walk to either. It seemed nice and also somehow familiar...

Then I began to think of all the unique things about this town. For example, everyone knew the day we moved in because we changed the garage doors. Those same people also usually mentioned that we must had a lot of furniture as they also saw 3 furniture trucks here...I let them down easy and let them know we also had cheap movers who were paid in steaks and beer.

It took me a while to get used to everyone also only using first names for people..."You know who you should call? Bill."...okay? Or just barely describing someone whose name you've forgotten, and only saying, "You know, the lady with the long hair who smiles..." and immediately they know of who you are speaking. Amazing. NOW, my fault, I can never remember any one's name, but I'm working on it, or I'll never survive!

Then it dawned on me, I live 'there'. You know the place. That place in a movie or TV show that you always associate the words quaint, quiet, and quirky. My TV place was from pretty much the best TV show made, Gilmore Girls. Yes, I live in the real life version of Stars Hollow. We have the tree lined streets, the people who drive by your house and see you outside and wave, and you've never met. You can buy guns at the florist, I'm really wanting to check that out. We even have Amish in the area, and you know that ups the "Super- Beautiful-Quaint-Little-Town" status. And I dare you to not wave at them, I'm not sure why, but it seems to be an unconscious motion when you see a horse and buggy.

The thing that I am saving for the best is the people. The people of Canton MO, have taken us under their wing, in such a caring and kind way. Dropping things off, and sort of looking after us from a far. There are not words to describe it, other than meant to be. We are so very blessed to be in this town! I'm so very glad to say that I live 'there'.

**...courage...**

**_Courage_**: the quality of mind or spirit that enables a person to face difficulty, danger, pain, etc., without fear; bravery.

Let me tell you, I probably should look into a career in acting, as for the last two weeks I have put on a fairly good front- I'm "frontin'" as they might say. I am able to bury quite a lot, turn it off as it may be when necessary. Who wants to see an ugly cry? So, I try to rise above, but lately my abilities are waning...

...even though the last couple of days have been, well, tough...I'm not giving up. It seems that just about the time I'm talking to a total stranger, the UGLY CRY tries to get out. Yesterday, it was at the license branch. Out of nowhere I JUST STARTED THE UGLY CRY. I quickly recovered. While she wasn't being intrusive at all, I congratulated her for being the first stranger I broke down crying in front of. I also told her there was no prize. Today, it was in front of an insurance sales woman, who of course I'd never met. Thankfully, even though I was quiet, it was a small office and someone in a cubical on the other side of the room came and gave me a Kleenex. She told me she was honored to be the second stranger to have cried in front of, which made me know she was good people.

Let's face it, I didn't have a fighting chance today to keep it together. Today was the first school program of the year. I sat there, speaking telepathically to Abe (doubtful he got the vibes), hoping he knew that Jason was watching him. Hoping he would be thinking of who was there instead of who wasn't. Sad, but not wanting to show it in any way possible. It's just the first of many firsts without Jason, and I'll figure it out. The original intent of this blog wasn't to go on about an ugly cry. Courage, right? My kids, all of them down to the 9 month old HAVE IT!

The start of school here was what you'd call interesting. The boys have worn uniforms for the last couple of years. Little did I know that going to public school would not only mean LIBERATION, but also mean a walk on a runway every day? I'm talking about the boys? It started with buying a "new-non-uniform-school-outfit". I let the boys pick out what they wanted, figuring they'd pick something fairly simple. It wasn't until Oscar picked out a pair of 'skinny jeans' that I began to get worried.

I was quickly, fervently, trying to PUSH any other pant in the whole store. I could just hear Jason saying, "What in the?!" But I thought, he'll try them on, and realize wearing a wet suit isn't very comfortable.

WRONG. He LOVED THEM. I'm not talking, felt okay, I'm talking LOVE. Immediately he started doing lunges, telling me how great they were. Frantically, I tried to think, I knew Jason wouldn't be down with the JEGGINGS. So, I told him if he wanted them, he'd have to buy them himself, and he did. While I was surprised at his choice, as he is built JUST LIKE JASON-well, and me at that age- I was impressed with his courage to try something new. New school, new style. Well, I use the term style loosely. It took both boys about a month to understand that you can't wear every print you OWN all at the same time.

The couple days following Jason's passing, Oscar came down stairs and announced to me, "I'm wearing my 'skinny jeans' for Dad...and I also think we need to eat thin crust pizza once a week to honor his memory". I couldn't help but think that Jason was not only smiling, but probably laughing his tail off.

### ...not sure if pissed is a bad word...

...I'm so very angry. I'm so very, very angry right now. No, I'm not. I'm pissed off. I sit here and rack my brain about every minute I shared with Jason. Every moment that I might not have appreciated. All the things that we will never share again. All the things that he won't see...

He hated snow. I was so looking forward to seeing the first snow fall on our house and snuggling with him (the only real reason he tolerated snow...not that snow gets me frisky or anything). He liked Christmas, but working retail, he was adamant that it not begin until the day after Thanksgiving, or even later. Never-the-less, it always cracked me up that he got 'giddy' at the notion of getting the Christmas dishes out...which makes me a little less pissed off when I think of it.

He loved old movies, and I have made it a mission for the next 4 days to record (on TMC only as there are no commercials-his very strict rule) any ones that were his favorites, to watch with the kids. He loved Thanksgiving, for the turkey, potatoes and pumpkin pie. Every couple of years we were able to be extra thankful as his birthday fell on that day as well like tomorrow. Probably contributes to me being pissed off...

I know. I know I have a long road ahead of me. I know I should probably take up drinking/crocheting/cleaning/cooking, anything to keep me busy, or away from this keyboard. To be honest, I'm hoping the action of getting it out on this keyboard will somehow free me of my anger. In some way it will take the 80 pound weight that is on my heart away. I know this Windows 8 laptop can do a lot, but...

I've tried to keep my emotions under wraps in front of my kids. Finding that if we can talk about funny stories, no one has to get bummed out. We might even learn something new. I did get caught getting teary the other day in front of Nora. She looked at me and said, "Mommy, you know, it's alright to be sad, we all miss Daddy..." I just got consoled by a 3 yr. old, bless her GIGANTIC HEART.

...but the whole thing brings to mind a story about one of the first Thanksgiving I ever spent with Jason. I told this story to the boys today. Personally, it is one of my favorite 'first' stories about Jason. It was the first time I visited Quincy. His Grandparents were also visiting as well. His Grandmother had begun to suffer from Alzheimer's, nothing severe, but noticeable. She had obviously been for a manicure before they came for a visit. <u>Every</u> time she saw Jason, she would stand back, and put her hands out, as if to show off her bright red nails. Every time she did this to Jason, he would not only compliment her on them, he never said the same thing twice. Never tired, always finding some way to make her feel beautiful. This was Thanksgiving 1995. I knew right then and there, I wanted to marry this man, if he was ever crazy enough to ask me.

While this is just one of many memorable stories about Jason, and while it doesn't help me miss him any less, I had one heck of man. For that this Thanksgiving, I have to be thankful...and maybe a little pissed...

### ...buck up Charles Schultz...

There are few things that say the holidays to my family and I like Charles Schultz. My kids, and well I, adore the holiday 'Charlie Brown' movies. Some civilizations strive on certain things, my family lives for October to begin the CHARLIE BROWN TRILOGY...

Now, I have to be honest, we don't mess around. We don't watch said movies on NETWORK TELEVISION...I shudder. We (thanks to my mother-in-law) own the box set. Any mother reading this? It is worth EVERY PENNY. All the Peanuts Gang you want, no commercials, and 30 minute show doesn't last an hour...no thanks needed, just a tip from me to you.

We don't watch these shows willy-nilly. No Great Pumpkin in June. No Thanksgiving movie in March. These movies are month specific: Great Pumpkin starts October 1st, and can be watched up to October 30th. Charlie Brown Thanksgiving can be watched in November, possible start date the 10th or so. Then we have to spread out the trilogy for the big finale, Charlie Brown Christmas from December 1st on.

The memories of the boys on our bed in their footie P.J.s, heads in hand watching, so little, and cute. The 'Talls' (Oscar and Abe) and I literally know them word for word. We each have our own favorite parts, certain parts that no one talks during as to not miss a funny part...we basically need a support group.

So, a week and a half ago, I realize that while we have had the Great Pumpkin experience, we hadn't even cracked open November's Charlie Brown favorite. Hoping in my heart of hearts, at least we can watch this, and keep something 'normal' (I use quotes as we are working thru the uncomfortable normal now). As I'm watching, I'm also watching my kids watching something we always found funny, fun, and a family thing. I'm watching them, sort of getting annoyed, slightly becoming over critical of their reactions. The fact that Atticus wouldn't sit still, Nora talked through the whole thing (shocker). Generally things weren't the FREAKING HAPPY TIMES we had always had! Hello? Why did I expect a giant Peanuts Gang Band-Aid to solve all our lives problems?

...it was then it hit me. This is A LOT of pressure to put on a guy! How was Charles Schultz supposed to fix this problem? He'd helped Charlie Brown every time, but then again, the kid never changes his clothes. So, Charles Schultz, buck up! We change our clothes, we don't have a cooking dog and we are coming back from this, one holiday at a time...

## Twelve step program or a cocktail party?

"...if you need anything, just call me..."
I have been blessed to hear these words
countless times in the last 3 weeks. People
whom I've known for years or those who I
have just met on the steps of my church. I
am in awe of humanity. Humbled and
overwhelmed by an out pouring of people
who want to help me. But here is the
question? Why can't I ask for help?

Why didn't I set up a system years ago?
Making sure that my husband and I had a
MANDITORY once a week date, even if it
were to go grocery shopping? Why didn't I
go out on more girl's nights? No weekends
away? None. Why am I so bad at asking for
help?

Well, first of all I have a slight diagnosis of
OCD. I equate that to someone coming into
your home and rearranging your clothes
while you were gone...how would you find
anything? And why the hell didn't they do it
your way? You had it all written down, in
your neatest handwriting, color coded and
broken down hourly as to what your kids
needed? Okay, so more than slight case.

I guess what I am trying to muddle through here is, when do you know you need help? When/how do you set that up when you have a 9 month old, a 3 year old, a 6 year old and an 8 year old? Sadly, even though I've had offers, the one person I'd want to go out with (after the day I've had none of the above mentioned are on my short list to leave the house with me), I can't...there's the rub.

Then I contemplate at certain times of day… What would it look like if I had someone come over, only for me to go down to check out the floral/gun shop and then go drinking alone? I also wonder, is there a club of women/widows out there who'd like to drink in the middle of the day, but can't leave the house because their kids are napping? I need a handbook. Until then, I am still very grateful for any and all offers of help. And while I openly admit I will need it, give me some time, I have to first learn how to ask...

## ...same but different...

...so, I've decided that it is necessary to start some new traditions. I feel like something new has to start, to try to not only take our minds off of well, our minds. I'm hoping if we have something "happy" to remember, it'll make this time of year sting a little less each year. Again, I have no idea what I am doing...

The blessing is that we are in a new house and new town brimming with holiday cheer! I was already told by the "truth-seeker", Oscar, that we will not be watching Rudolf until December 1st. He sort of has me over a barrel and has figured out that 'Santa' is not only not real, but thought everyone should know the truth. I quickly quelled his interest in crapping on every one's Christmas. I explained that Santa isn't any one person, but many people who want something magical to believe in, especially children. Now he was in on that little secret. Also, if he ruined this magical belief for anyone else in this house, he would only be opening old man underwear on Christmas.

With every growing day, it is apparent to me why we are here. I don't mean on this earth, but here in this little town and house. I can't imagine how much more difficult it would be right now living in our old house, reminding us with every step who was missing from our daily lives, regardless that he will always be in our heavy hearts. Sometimes when I feel like I want to give up, I am reminded how much Jason loved this house. At times it's almost liberating to know that we can start any new tradition we want. I'm still trying to figure all this out, but I feel like he is helping me in some cosmic way...

Thankfully, my children are all different. They all have their own way of communicating, which is good and worrisome at the same time. Last night, finally, one of the boys decided to open up. I was surprised however at what he opened up about. All this time I have been trying to gently talk about Jason every day. Asking them questions, bringing up funny stories or nicknames. It never occurred to me that one of their woes would have been, what if something happens to me? After 3 weeks of, well, slightly expected hellish behavior. Knowing that at least but not limited to once a day, they mentally plotted my death, angry that their dad was no longer here. I'm not delusional, I know that this will continue. However, it never occurred to me, even with this anger, they were worried about losing me. Moreover, the most fascinating thing is how differently my kids process what they are feeling. It's mind boggling and keeps me guessing...like I need one more thing to do. But it is great to know that while we might not all be feeling the same thing, we are still feeling something.

So, as December 1st is almost upon us, the Elf on the Shelf will be here...German and Lego Advent gifts...crafts...hot chocolate...cookies...parade of lights and a treasure trove of movies begin. Through all this, I will be listening for Jason, and wishing for many reasons that he were still here...possibly cursing, daily, for the damn Elf on the Shelf placement!

**...the new options...**

Jason used to tell me, "You look fine in whatever you wear, you don't have to dress to impress others..." While I always appreciated him saying that, I have noticed most of the things I did or wear day to day was for him. Now what?

I'm not one to wear much make-up, Jason used to tell me that I didn't need it. Although, I always thought it was funny when I slapped a little on he would say, "Well, don't you look nice..." I have made it 3 weeks wearing nothing, partly because I don't want to, partly because I have no idea when the flood gates will open. Figuring usually better safe than sorry. But the whole thing got me thinking, what else do I not have to do?

I made a joke with my bestie April, just after Jason passed, saying it just dawned on me, I'm going to save a fortune in razors. Maybelline and L'Oreal will not be seeing me in their aisles. Victoria Secret will no longer need my business for thongs. I no longer have to try to look like a "vixen" when going to bed...well, my interpretation of a vixen. It's now whatever I am wearing and socks. Hot.

However, I found out quick what my kids pay attention to. For example, you DO NOT use Dad's coffee mug. I learned that the first day. I was wanting to use it, as it is one Jason always used. Frankly, I had no idea they would even notice. Wrong. I made a mental note, and went on. It seems however at this point in time, there is a lot of thinking what we will never get to do with Jason again. I was severely guilty of this in the beginning I have made a vested attempt to try to stop that way of thinking. My Abe however, isn't there yet. I know he is going to come through this, but the fact that I can't take-away what he is feeling, as a mother, is hard. And, at this point, I am waiting for him to say, "Yeah, well, I don't care how you are feeling, this is how I'm feeling!!!"

While I miss him every minute of the day, I am blessed with the notion that my boys will grow to be great men because of Jason. They will each have, in their own way, the very best qualities of him. They (as well as myself) are also blessed to have his friends for support. Those gentlemen that knew Jason when, and were STILL friends with him up till the end...thank you.

It seems that my family grew immeasurably on November 7, 2012, and I am thankful for that. And the fact that if I never want to shave my legs, wear a thong, look "sexy", wear make-up, or generally just keep myself up, I don't have to. That's not to say I don't miss it...

### ...why you CRAY-CRAY?

...Mom?...Mom?...Mom?...Mom?...Mom?...
hey, Mom?...hey,
Mom?...Mommy?...MOM?!?!...

And most of these are when I am sitting
directly next to one of my kids. I have
decided that at some point, I will only
answer to Francine. Still I ponder, why do
they have to say MOM if we are the only
people in the room? And clearly I'm sitting
on the same couch...

So, I have come to a conclusion: Anyone
who has four kids, on their own, by choice,
with no live in nanny, just doing it alone? Is
a masochist...chemically
imbalanced...starting a kiddie work
camp...CRAY-CRAY! Why in the world
would you want to do ALL OF THIS
WORK ALONE? Or maybe they weren't
blessed with someone in their lives that was
ever on their team, and at the end of the day
(well, let's face it any time of day) I miss my
team mate...

There I am, at the breakfast table, and
everyone, EVERYONE, is singing a

different Christmas song, at the top of their lungs. I can remember when they would get more than a little loud, and that was Jason's wake up call. He'd walk down the hall, all bed head and slit eyed and mumble and then shout, "WELL, GOOD MORNING!!!" All the kids would laugh! Sometimes I wonder on mornings like today, if the kids sort of catch themselves after no one comes down the hall...

Sundays are my new challenge. Thankfully, church isn't until 10:30. We can walk there, and we usually make it with Nora falling down once and me telling the boys not to run. From there, it's a full contact sport-holding Atticus at this point in his life. I feel should be an Olympic sport. Degree of difficulty? Way the hell harder than curling, just in front of badminton. Whispering to Nora, "No, we just got here, it isn't over yet..." Making sure the boys are at least pretending we are in church and not in a locker room. All the while finding the solace that I made it there, in one piece and maybe Jesus could take my "wheel" for the next hour? No? Okay...

But today, while wrestling a 9 month old it hit me? Embrace the madness. EMBRACE

IT! Yes, this whole thing sucks. Yes, this is not how you wanted your life. Yes, the noise is deafening. Yes, your house needs cleaned. Yes, you have no idea where the rest of the day will take you, so embrace it. You will no doubt lose your temper, not talking 'Mommy Dearest' here, but you will slip. You will realize that the chaos that is sometimes 4 kids in one room would scare the lame to walk again. You are wearing clean underwear, and so are your kids. You will have "peaks and valley" days, but why not end it with an ice cream sandwich?

Doesn't that make sense? You live in madness, you have to deal with it, and you have ice cream. Not sure if that is some hidden equation to how I need to live my life for a while, but having a 3 year old make my cocktail seems a little inappropriate, so I'll take it.

**...Mr. Sandman...**

**...*dream*: a succession of images, thoughts, or emotions passing through the mind during sleep...**

So, for four weeks I have been asking. For four weeks I have pleaded nightly, stayed awake to be extra tired, to just dream. To dream about Jason, talk to him, connect in a way that I so badly need. Just he and I.

The morning after he passed, I was filled with an unconscionable rage as I heard my Dad say, "Jason popped into my dream last night..." I looked at my Dad, chin quivering, eyes filled with tears, as he explained how he talked to Jason in his dream. Why him? He's never seen Jason naked...cleaned his underwear...loved/longed for him as much as I did. It begs me to ask, when will it be my turn?

Nora has had a dream, where he laid down with her and talked. Talked about the things she liked to do and told her that he would bring her pink flowers. At first I figured this was just some machination, created in her overly verbal brain to bring up during her never ending small talk sessions. But, the fact that she re-accounts the same thing every time we talk about him, our nightly routine, makes me think that maybe Jason has blessed her little brain with a visit. The interesting thing about dreaming and Jason, is that he marveled at the fact that he rarely did dream. When he did, they were these hilarious scenarios where he was attacking a bat the size of a cat in our house or that he was in a scene from the movie *Red Dawn*. You know, things you could really put into daily perspective. Such was Jason, while he was at times quiet, his brain moved faster than the speed of light. Only when he was really hot on a topic, did he let you have it, always however, respecting the others opinion. It's just who he was...what I miss.

The whole thing makes me also wonder...maybe he doesn't think I can handle it? Maybe he is hiding from me nightly because he is worried that it is just too soon...too much...too tough. I've heard of other widows, months after their loved ones have passed, having very vivid dreams. At times, questioning if it were a dream or an actual visit from beyond. I'm not asking to play out a scene from *Ghost*, just want to somehow connect, if only for a brief moment, to get me over the hurdle in the race I am now running called life. I'm trying to train my brain to believe that when he thinks I need him, he will appear...

So, my sojourn continues. I will keep praying/pleading/begging to just see him one more time in my dreams...if for only a moment more of, well, him.

**...broken things can be fixed...**

So, you'd think after 8 years of parenting, four kids, and all that goes along with it, I'd learn...before I clicked "order" on amazon, or mentioned lists to Grandparents, I'd have remembered the things kids really want for Christmas...

Now, the older kids get, the MORE they 'need' at Christmas. Jason and I realized this a few years ago and had made it our mission to make sure our kids knew the difference between 'needing' and 'wanting'. Our hope was that along the way they'd also learn from this the idea of being grateful for what they already have. However, many know how this time of year the "GREEDIES" rear their ugly head, and that is a whole different blog all together...

The fact of the matter is, before I ordered/bought anything for Nora, I should have gone to the dollar store and picked up 3 things. The other day she was rewarded with a 25cent yo-yo from Old Navy. It was quickly THE THING she played with (subsequently, it was also the thing I wound up about 400 times, but I digress). You know the old adage, your kid gets this super awesome gift from a distant relative and you find yourself saying, "Yes, Aunt Martha, your gift was perfect, they are playing with the box it came in as we speak..."

But today, even after St. Nick left a few goodies for Nora, it was the 25 cent yo-yo that she was playing with, that is until it broke (in reality, it lasted about 24 hours longer than I thought it would). She immediately came running into the kitchen pleading with me to fix it. As all 25 cent toys go, I figured I would lower the boom early, that I probably couldn't fix it. To which she said, "But mom, broken things can be fixed..."

This got me thinking...if she only knew. If she only knew that not all broken things can be fixed. It was an often discussed topic, Jason's kidney transplant in 2000 was not a cure, just a means to an end. And he was always one to point out to me that he would never out live me. I would scoff these statements off, mainly as a defense mechanism. But also because I would never want to even ponder the notion of life without him. But life, much like the 25 cent yo-yo, cannot be "fixed" now, no matter how broken some moments of the day feel.

So now, a month into this new life for us, we are finding rewards in other things. Folding the laundry in the morning while quizzing kids on spelling words, Nora is nearly there, spelling 'dog' Z-O-J. Getting the TALLS out the door to school with a minimum of arguing....a steady daily diet of *Jacks Big Music Show* / *Sesame Street* (praise the Lord for a DVR!). Surviving the day without anyone limping...homework done, dinner done, prayers and bedtime...we made it...

While none of this might compare to a 25 cent yo-yo for Nora, I am finding courage/resolve in the notion that we are keep-on-keeping-on even though we might be a little broken...

**...yes, I want mayo on that BLT...**

So, tonight we went out for the first time in a month together, sans the drool box (Atticus), all to see the Canton Parade of lights. While the parade was fun and took me back to my childhood of living in a little town like Canton, the dinner show was what I will remember, for a while...

We went to a little sandwich/pizza/ice cream shop that we'd never been to before. Of course, Oscar had to walk about 10 paces ahead, as not to be seen with us. Abe immediately saw someone he knew and had to do some strange hand jive with the kid. And Nora, well, she acted as though she'd lost her hearing aid, forever losing her inner volume.

Nora, sat right down, hadn't even taken off her coat, and announced that she would be having "PANCAKES". I told her that I didn't think this place served those to which she said okay. Then the waitress appeared and asked what we'd like to drink, to which Nora said, "Yes, I'll be having the pancakes!" After settling on a cheese sandwich and a Sierra Mist, the floor show began with a rousing 'songbook' of every song she has ever learned. All the while, making sure to make eye contact with everyone around her whilst singing, as though they were tipping tonight.

Abe, who should probably run for mayor of Canton someday, knew about a half dozen people who walked in. To which his reputation as "...The Most Interesting Man in the World..." had him shooting winks to all he knew while simultaneously saying,

"Hey there, how you doing?" However, the best line he delivered, and one I will remember for a few months, is when a kid from his school walked by and Abe leaned over and said, "Hola, Amigo..." huh? Oscar asked him, "...does he speak Spanish?" To which Abe said, "...what? I don't know..."

Oscar, well, let's face it, we were bringing down his reputation. You have very little "street cred" when the people you are with are all wearing Santa hats. The kid must be growing as he ate his meal and half of Abe's. I do find it funny that he will read an entire menu, cover to cover, to announce that he would be having a BLT...you have to weigh your options bud.

The parade was bigger than I expected and even though we weren't patient enough to wait for Santa, we did some aggressive waving and cheering for him. Nora got to hug him as he walked past us. We were lucky enough to run into our neighbors and then some more friends we knew. All and all, I'd hoped to start a tradition in this great little town and had the best time just watching my kids!

**...with great power, comes great responsibility...**

...I am amazed. I am daily amazed at women. I feel like I am just carrying around the parts, of which make me such, and maybe I will be able one day to be one of these, women...

Now, I'm not going to lie, I have felt like one of these women after I gave birth to my first child. There is just something about it, afterward you feel like you need to be interviewed as if you just climbed Everest. Your face should be on a Wheaties box, or somehow highlighted on ESPN (probably would be a lot less men watching if that were the case). You want to tell every person you see, "I made THAT!!" And if you are lucky enough, you will see it, that awe in the eyes of your husband. That will be enough. Cancel my interview with ESPN.

At times these women come into our lives when we need them. Like cloaked super heroes, swooping in, saving the day, and moving on to the next person in peril. They do not need acknowledgement for what they do, just the deed, in and of itself, is enough.

My husband would tell me I was one of these people. Sadly, while I always appreciated it, I've always fancied myself as a **side-kick**...usually his. Now, I find myself sort of lost. What the devil did Robin do without Batman? You never saw, ONE Wonder-Twin. Maybe she grew up to be Wonder Woman? But, that is no longer an option, and it is time to pay it forward, and take a lesson from these WOMEN...

I am forever changed by these women that can take on anything. These women who will lay down their life for the good of many, or just their own, whatever. I am forever graced to know women like these, humbled by their actions, their courage, their strength. With any luck, I can gain strength from them. These women don't ask questions, they just do. They don't always care about the rules, they just know what is right. They are women.

I am blessed to have been able to realize that not only do I know women like this, I know A LOT of women like this. While a few weren't there on Monday night, the women I spent Monday night with are these WOMEN (luckily for me, there are too many to mention). These WOMEN who I am forever indebted to. These WOMEN who came together to help my family. These WOMEN who some I knew, others I did not, but all I have the fortune of saying are now my friends. They are these women who inspire me...to be me. Thank you for giving others the strength they need, you WOMEN...

## ...get the" funk" out

...in a funk. What is a funk? Where in the world did that word come from? There are many different kinds, I know that much...wishing right now, I was in a "funk" about not knowing what to wear...Or in a "funk" about what to make for dinner. The "funk" I'm in is something more....

Maybe the antibiotics I am on aren't working properly. Having a swollen face and an aching jaw could put a girl in a "funk". However, I am thinking this is just compounded by, well, my life. Mentally crossing off all the **things** I need to do on a day to day basis. Some so that this palace isn't taken over by vermin. Some so that we all have clean underwear (the frantic worry of a mother, no clean underwear). Some **things** on this mental check list are those I've never had to worry about before, and still others are now **things** to keep my mind from actually thinking. Thinking about what has been, and what's to come, and who's not here...the reason for my funk.

I've never been a competitive sports player, I sort of feel like my current day-to-day has now entered that realm. Keeping my eye on the prize (currently, not bawling in front of strangers). Psyching myself for the competition, knowing that my strength will push me when I need it, and questioning that at the same time. Picturing the finish line, and hoping to make it there in one piece. Wearing clean underwear, in a clean-ish house, everyone safe and sound. All to earn my prize, go to sleep, and do it all over again in the morning. I guess more like a mouse in a maze instead of a sports player...

I tell myself in the quiet of each morning (yes that does happen, though it is EARLY and dark outside), that I am so very blessed to be in the situation I am in. I have these unique, beautiful children, who are loving and thoughtful. And regardless of their current situation, they are blooming into these interesting, curious beings. While they have a lot of me in them, they have the very best part of what is missing in their lives in them as well. For that, I not only **have to** keep going, but I owe it to myself to see how the story of their lives will play out...and, the "funk" is gone...at least for now...

## ...knowing when to shut it down...

...lately, there have been things that have caught me funny. I don't mean things that make me just smile, I mean laugh out loud whenever you think about them. Maybe it's a defense mechanism. Perhaps my brain is trying to level out my hormones/emotions/or the just plain CRAZIES. In which case, thank you brain. At this point in my life I know all of my kid's birth dates, but currently cannot remember my pin number on the debit card I've had for 11 years...

For example, the other day I picked up a prescription for whatever the crap attacked my face/sinuses. I find it funny, I could walk into the walk-in clinic with a severed leg, and they would check my eyes, poke my

arm...and give me Amoxicillin. I felt like I
was in college again. I am seriously battling
whatever it is I have. I pull out of the drive-
thru pharmacy whilst opening up the
prescription to get the meds in me. As I open
it up I read: This drug may interfere with
your birth control...I almost wrecked my car
laughing...

I have found that these such things cannot be
helped, and sometimes people are stupid and
have to be shut down. A bill
collector/payment assistant called Jason's
phone as I was at the cell phone store getting
all of his contacts/photos etc. transferred to
my phone. His phone had basically been
turned off for 3 weeks, and suddenly it rings.
The person on the other line was a tad
annoyed and immediately was on 10, when
he should have been about 3 on the tension
scale. I let him rant on for a minute and I
said, "Well, do you have any idea that the
number you have been calling for the last 3
weeks was that of my deceased husband?
Furthermore, did you know that not only do
we have insurance, but we haven't even
asked for assistance?" Meanwhile, the jaw
of the little gal who was helping me I could
have picked up off of the floor. Admittedly,
I had hit my mental wall that day, and sadly,

he should have checked his facts before trying to verbally wrestle with me.

Then there are times when you laugh, knowing that all of the things you have feared for the last 186 hours, are for not. All the things you want to fix, but don't know how, are alright and at the moment don't require mending. While the ironic laugh is appreciated, laughing at this could easily be mixed with tears, just knowing its one less thing to worry about for the moment. At times like this, I think of Jason and figure he's clocked in, working.

They say grief comes in waves. It sounds weird, but in reality, it's the only way to describe what it's like. OR I've figured out it's sort of like being pregnant and dealing with hormones. You could be going along fine, getting thru your day like it is any other. And then the Hy-Vee ad comes. Seeing that Hy-Vee add you are reminded of something you used to buy for a favorite dinner. It's like you are hearing an ambulance come by your house. You can hear it in the distance, you know it's coming, and the tension builds, as the noise gets louder and louder. Finally, it's in front of you and you see it, and then it's past your house and down the road, and then gone.

While I was pregnant, I used to laugh, because it was ridiculous and couldn't be controlled and you just had to let it "happen". Clearly, waves is easier to explain, but I'm chatty so what are you going to do?

One of these 'waves' came today, but not out of me rather my 3 year old. I'd imagine it was a mixture of being tired, bored, and well, brilliant (I'm a mom, I have to brag when they do something right to counteract when they misspell something they've spray painted on the side of a building later). I find it fascinating that my Nora can openly talk about almost anything. She can carry on a conversation like an 8 year old, and **at times** during the day I am grateful for this. Today, she was sitting on my lap and turned to me and said, "Mommy, I love you, but my heart is breaking. I miss Daddy so much..."

Well...well...wow. I told her I felt the same way. I told her that our hearts are going to hurt for a while. But I was so glad I had her to love and fill in the cracks of my heart. Of all the kids, she is the most open. Wanting to talk, not afraid to ask questions, no matter how many times she asks the same question. And no, he can't come back...No matter how many times she asks. I'm grateful she is asking, knowing that with time, these questions will be answered in her little brilliant brain.

Even after a CRAZY day, at the end I'm finding I am able to at least glean something positive out of it. Whether it be putting the 'littles' to bed a little early-even though knowing my day might start that much earlier. Or being able to get a few things done or talk to an adult while the boys are at CCD-that's priceless! Chatting with the 'talls' about life, freezer-burn and the grocery list. And doing this, just the act of writing, to clear my head at the end of the day. While I might not always be laughing in the moment, at least I can try again later...

**Haters going to Hate**

...Jason used to say, "Love your 'Haters', because when they stop hating, you know you are not doing a good job...if they are hating on you, go on and do your thing, haters are going to hate..."

When the haters are beings you birthed into this world, it stings a little more. By no means am I surprised at the notion that currently (hopefully only for a little while) my kids have a tad bit of hate in them. Thankfully, not all of them, which gives me a glimmer of hope that maybe somehow, some way, they can learn from one another how to deal with their loss. Clearly anything I have discussed with them hasn't always been accepted, or even 'heard'. More over this dissension in the ranks, has made some of my kids realize a lot more about what they have, as well as what they have lost.

Now, I understand that a grieving person is like a snowflake, no two people deal the same way. However, this begs me to ask: when is it wrong to stop being hated? Women, we know other women who do this. When I was in the workforce, the one I had to leave my house for, Jason used to also ALWAYS say, "There are too many damn women working where you work...drama!" Some people thrive on it, and when you are in it it's hard to swim past it. At times while it is frustrating to be hated on, when you can spin it to be a back handed compliment, you sort of rise above it, nearly gaining strength from it.

But the 'hater' I have currently, well, it's tough. When the hate is confused, sad, and from someone who you love more than your life, it is heart wrenching. I was told about this, from one of my other teary eyed children, as if to tell me his heart broke with this notion as well. After talking it out, the first thing that played in my head, was the quote from Jason...it seems he's working his magic again, and I need to take notice and let the haters hate, be hopeful, and move on...


## ...pennies from heaven...

...what do you want for Christmas, Mom? I have been asked that question for about 20 days. With all the holiday whoopla going on around us, the school programs and parties...the stores BLARING all things Christmas...I am left feeling, blah. While the **magic** of this season is best seen in the eyes of a child, even my children are starting to resemble Ebenezer what's his name at times...and I can't help but think I might be to blame.

Each child, excluding Atticus, has taken to humming Christmas music. At times I find unnerving, but I figure it's like free depression medication, and if it helps, I'm ALL FOR IT. All their songs vary. Abe has a songbook of songs he likes the best, and hums/sings at odd times. Oscar hums all year round, usually the theme music to Harry Potter or Star Wars. Nora, well, I almost fell over when I overheard her singing the other day. Out of nowhere, she started belting out, "...*every time it rains, it rains, PENNIES FROM HEAVEN, shoo-bee-doo-bee*..." From that point on, I figured, if you want to hum, sing, or just make happy noise (as long as it can be tolerable), DO IT!

A dear friend sent us an early Christmas gift on Saturday. She described this person as a 'realistic Santa,' I wondered how realistic could he be? Well. Wow! Abe answered the door (by the way, if a crazed gunman ever takes us out, probably because Abe let him in the door, just saying') to which this giant man, dressed in the most beautiful red suit, trimmed with bright white soft fur, said, "Abe, how are you doing' my boy?!" Abe looked at Oscar, as if to say, "HA! I TOLD YOU HE WAS REAL!!!" I have never actually seen someone mentally crap their pants, however, I resisted the urge to ask Oscar if he needed to change his undies!

Nora was so, well, star struck! Besides asking him if he wanted to see her room, she started making up things about herself to discuss with him. At one point I heard her tell him she did ballet and was a ballerina? This giant Santa, came in, knew all the kids names, sat in our living room, answered questions, and had each child sit on his lap and tell him what they wanted for Christmas. The very best part was that the kids could get so close and see this man, his beard, this hair, his belly, was all real...they could see the **magic**.

The 'Talls' and I had a long chat about Christmases past last night. Year by year, what I got at what age etc. It was interesting, while I couldn't recall the last 36 Christmases in detail, the ones I did remember we laughed about. I found it odd that they asked if I got bras for my 13th Christmas...I don't want to know the innermost thoughts of boys, yuck. But in talking to them, I understood why they were asking me all these questions. They wanted to know about my magic, my magical memories Christmases past...the simple act of asking me, to me, was magic.
In Christmases past, I would always ask Jason what he'd want for Christmas. He'd say, "Nothing, I have it already..." to which I

would say, "Well you have to open something..." Having a birthday 5 days after Christmas, I always felt like I had to bring it home with what I wanted, because it's a whole year until I get this chance again. But this year, it's a little different. A couple of months ago I could have thought of a dozen things I might have wanted, but didn't need...they all seem, well, stupid now. The list of frivolous THINGS, seem slightly shadowed by what my heart wants/needs/aches for.

I have been given my Christmas gifts. This beautiful house, that looks even more magical when decorated for Christmas. My children, who while they add to the grey hair count, like it or not, are giant gifts that not only couldn't be wrapped, but wouldn't fit under the Christmas tree...

Now, I know more than ever what Jason was talking about. While I always hoped he knew I felt the same way, now, it's all I think of when asked "what do you want for Christmas?"

**...In the year of the Dog...**

...not sure if it's the day long headache...the possible snow fall...the nearly 'there' with Christmas that is making my kids act like a bunch of speed addicts...the endless list of things to worry about. Tonight, for the first time in weeks, I could not stop crying or just wanting to cry
...childlike...credulous...ignorant...lamb... simpleminded...square...wide-eyed...all words that could also mean naive...the world I live in. I avert my eyes a lot. I keep moving, cleaning, and staying active so as not to have to actually think. I do all of these things to try to avoid really feeling. Avoid the inevitable emptiness that if I actually thought about it would not only tear me in half, but would also be so destructive. I sleep very little during the night, wish I could during the day, and pay for it the rest. I worry that if I stare too long at any one picture of him that is when I will fall apart.

I talk a good game. People ask how I am doing, and instinctively I know the pre-programed answer I will give. Taking into consideration the day of the week, weather, or time of day. I'm like those fortunes on the place mats at the Chinese restaurant. Today I'll give you the year of the dog, tomorrow might be the rabbit. I don't mean any disrespect to those asking, let's face it, it's a no win question, with an even less desirable answer. But at least they care enough to ask, and they will be prosperous in love as well as in their business endeavors...

I literally will be standing at the kitchen sink, doing dishes and out of the clear blue sky it hits me...as if the last 6 weeks didn't happen...like I just stumbled upon a bad *Lifetime* movie... it dawns on me, he isn't coming back. He's not visiting friends in another state. He's not working late. He's not out watching the game somewhere...he isn't coming back. It is at that point when I feel ignorant, simple minded, and heartbroken...why can't my heart and my head be reading the same book? Why do I have to be **reminded** that he isn't coming back...like I needed that?

I find it interesting that I can have the appropriate answer to the question of "How ya doing?", but I can't convince myself of my answers. Why can't I take my own advice? I know why, because at this point I can't even take any one's advice. When I find myself sad or angry about life, for whatever reason, everything that has been

said to me that I dread is all that fills my
head. Knowing this holiday is going to be,
well, sucky. Knowing that my kids have to
work thru all of this in their own time.
Hoping that one day, it doesn't have to be
even in the next year, I'll wake up and not be
terrified of where our lives will go...sort of
like someone telling you to strap on
those lead boots and jump in the pool.

I want to try. I want to hope. I wish I could
tell my head, that there is no way that I have
forgotten Jason. There is no possibility that I
do not miss every single thing about him.
There is no way that I have forgotten my
very best friend. I want to tell my head that
having to be reminded hurts. Having to be
reminded makes me sick to my stomach,
weak and a shell of myself. I want to tell my
head that I am reminded at 4:45 am when I
am feeding Atticus...or at 6:15 am when
giving Nora and Atticus a bath (and Jason
would have laughed as Atticus has found his
manhood and is quite fascinated with the
whole thing-water magnifies and all)...or at
6:25 when Oscar came in the bathroom,
greeted us, proceeded to take a whiz and
fart...or Abe coming in shortly after asking,
"What are ya all doin'?" Really? Is the
bathroom confusing? I don't need reminders
that tear me down. My day is so full of

reminders **Post-It** is calling me for tips...but you could drop by a girl in her dreams…that I'd take...

## ...where's Burl Ives when you need him...

Going 75 miles an hour down highway 61 yesterday, Nora in the back seat scream/singing *Jingle Bells*, as if she is being paid. While I laugh I'm also trying to bury something someone has said that I cannot get out of my mind "...you should know, this holiday season will be hard..."

Really? That's the best you can do? Someone had to actually mention this to me, as if I didn't already know? As if I actually thought the tree, Santa, Christmas music, Advent gifts, baking, Christmas lights and snow would somehow make all of this go away...

What I am really dreading is after Christmas...what is there to look forward to? Now, first I need to take a minute to thank and be thankful for the friends that I have. I HAVE THE BEST FRIENDS in the WORLD. Some people in this group I've known for years, but maybe haven't seen...some of these friends I have never met and somehow my family is on their heart this Christmas season.

My kids have been shown love. The love that they are missing and cannot put into words, and just love that is people wanting to make them smile, if only for a moment. My kids have had to understand more this Christmas than I ever wanted them to at their young age. Thankfully, I am blessed to have these FRIENDS that, even though my kids might have never met them, these friends love my kids as much as I do. There are no words to appropriately thank people, friends, like that.

Then there are friends that I have needed...the ones who write me a message, somehow mentally knowing that I am in need of building up. Being reminded that even though life hands you things you don't want to deal with, you have to, you will, and you are doing the best you can do. There aren't enough ways to thank you for doing this...it is thoughtfully read, contemplated, and greatly appreciated.

So, yes, I know this Christmas is going to be hard, but having said that I want to thank those I am blessed to know, my

FRIENDS, because of you, it is going to be survivable...

**...be sure to tell 'em, Large Marge sent ya...**

"...ah, fellas....I'm not sure I can do this....this is pretty high, and wow, it just goes straight down..."~me
"...what? ...sure we can, just sit down and let go..."~kids

For the first time in weeks, I feel like for a brief moment I let go...my kids let go...and we had a blast. We have been talking since we moved into this house that the hill on the next block that we can see from our house (the back end of Culver Stockton College) would be THE most perfect sledding hill ever. We have driven down the 'concourse,' as it is called, surveyed the hill, taking into consideration height and its lack of any obstacles. Velocity should have been brought into that as well...

The boys have been on me since the sight of the first snow flake, when will we sled??!!

Thankfully my mother-in-law was here, and we made the maiden trek to "The Big Hill" as it shall now be known. While walking to the top, I asked Nora, "Should we just stop here, and sled from this point?" To which Nora said, "Nope Mommy, we need to go to the top..."

The crisp wind in my face and the crunch of the snow underfoot... I sat down, more than slightly apprehensive, with my Nora-pie, watching the boys on their sleds. The sheer joy, mixed with a little nervous terror, on their face was something I will never forget. The squeals, the laughter, the excited shrieks of "WEEEEEEEE", all the way down...and then Nora and I got about 10 feet and wiped out. She wasn't fazed, she was ready to go again, all the while watching the boys zip by her at lightning speed and a grin on her and their faces! Round two ended sideways with me rolling over her. Snow up her nose, lost glove, and let's face it, FEAR halted her for a moment...
The boys, still sledding like they had done this a hundred times, were whipping by us laughing and trying to see if they could stay on their sleds.

I talked Nora into going halfway up the hill...a way less 'seeing-your-life-flash-before-your-eyes' sort of hill. Much better, and infinitely less terrifying for the both of us. She was filled with all of this nervous energy, she squealed and laughed and out of nowhere decides to yell..."BE SURE TO TELL 'EM, LARGE MARGE SENT YA!!!"...note: when your kids like random, and I do mean random movies, be ready to deal...I almost fell over laughing.

The complete release of all the stifled emotions, pent up feelings, basically CRAP that we have had to live with, was just let go...as if hurling down that hill (at this point I'm calling it a mountain because it's fragging high), freed us for a little while...the wind and snow in our faces sort of anointed us as carefree...I think as far as this winter goes, we might have found our free therapy...on The Big Hill...

**...so, you missed it, today was Christmas...**

...I woke up, just as normal, when Atticus wakes up. Today it was 4:15 for a diaper change, a bottle and then back to sleep for him...I had only been asleep for a few hours, dreading this day...wondering how much I would miss you...knowing I had to keep it together for our kids as this day was going to be hard enough missing you without having to look at their blubbering mother.

So, I figured, I would go at this day like any other, it's Tuesday, right? I folded laundry, made breakfast, emptied the dishwasher, made coffee, made bottles and waited...waited for the inevitable internal battle. I told the kids Merry Christmas, gave them a hug and kiss and appeared outwardly excited. I did all the things I always did every other Christmas...**trying** to make sure that this day was not any different than those in the past, but I'm not that talented.

I made it about 3 hours, the stockings and gifts were opened (very grateful for them, but you would have thought there were too many, and I would have agreed), paper thrown away, and everyone under 4 feet scurried off to their corners to explore their loot...but like I said, I made it 3 hours and got teary. Then an hour later, I put some boxes outside and went to the garage to really cry, scream, yell, and well just try to expel all that was inside. I **screamed** at you...I **screamed** at life...I **screamed** at the fact that I missed you so much and I didn't

WANT to do this without you...I didn't
WANT anything but for you to walk into the
room and wrap your arms around me and
hug me...my secret wish for Christmas. I'm a
masochist to want something I couldn't
actually get...I should have been happy with
pajamas.

I know I should be so happy to have what I
have. I know I should be so grateful to have
your children by my side. I know I should be
finding the treasures in all that are around
me instead of wishing for what I cannot
have, feel, or no longer see because you are
not here to make that all possible. While I
always knew it, I never appreciated that fact
that you were my 'charger'. When things got
stressful, tiresome, or just too much I would
look at you or go to you for a hug, and
magically I was better. Those mere acts,
made it all better...something so small that is
so tremendously missing for me...

So, on this first Christmas without you, I
know that you are watching over me. I so
deeply wish you were instead right beside
me, to look at my puffy, tear drenched eyes,
that have not so secretly mourned your
absence today…to smile at me give me a
hug and say, "You know, you look like shit,
go to bed..."...so, I guess that's what I'll do...

**...so, I'm partying like its 1995...**

So, Atticus went to bed early and we rang in the New Year...at 8pm. I'm no masochist...I value my private time, and I'm not about to find out what kids who stay up till midnight look like. We played games, had 'cocktails' and snacks and at 8 pm, we hugged each other, kissed each other, and told each other that we loved them. All and all, it was the kinder/gentler rendition of New Year's Eve, and we decided that we need to make it a tradition...maybe next year we'll add a few party go-ers too...

About 10 minutes before our 'new year' rang in, I was flushed with a memory of a New Year's Eve past...a night that I had forgotten at times, others I found it oddly interesting. Tonight I cherish it like a gift that never has to be put away...my first New Year's Eve with Jason...

It was December 31st 1995. Jason and I had only been dating for a couple of months and we were at a party in Muncie, Indiana. The regular New Year's Eve stuff going on, music, dancing, drinking, laughing and everyone crowding around a TV at the scant minutes before midnight. The countdown began, and you sort of held close those who you were with, looking at each other anxiously awaiting the ringing in of the New Year. I remember Jason kissing me, hugging me and whispering into my ear that he loved me and someday he would marry me.

At the time I probably thought, someone cut this man off, he's had too much...but it's the years that past that has made me treasure his comment, his possible insight into the life that we would call OURS. The possibility that perhaps you know, even years before it is meant to happen, that it's meant to happen. I find it oddly/longingly securing that he is who I was meant to be with...that while a girl's heart can tell her many things, sometimes fancifully, it was his heart that told the tale years before...

Somehow, I was given this great love...somehow I was found worthy of something so profound. Many people search for years, some settle for second best...but I was given this immense reward of not only being loved, but knowing love. Knowing how it can wrap you like a blanket, safe and warm...knowing that it can make your heart skip a beat even years after first meeting...knowing just the sound of a voice or a song can take you hypnotically back to that place, that time, when unconsciously you were waltzing right into the best thing that ever happened to you.

That being said, today, I sat at the end of my bed, in the middle of the day for about, well, as long as it takes to put on socks, talking to him. Crying. I am too busy to even know what the hell I'm doing most of the time, usually I get about a minute and a half to quietly lose it. Today it was to just sit for 134 seconds and cry to him...tell him that I need him...tell him that I don't want to do this alone...ask him for help. In the beginning, I saw little flashes of him...now, it's harder to spy them as there isn't enough quiet time of the day, or a crawling exploring baby to chase after...maybe these are new flashes? Like the saying that having children is many parents 'prayer'...when I want him, I'm at a loss. When I think need him, I'm at a loss...**but when he knows I need him, it's like him whispering into my ear so many years ago**...and there he is.

So, on this last day of one of the toughest years of my life, I look forward (with a little silent terror) to what life has in store for me...I pray those I know will hold close the ones they love...hug a little tighter, kiss a little more fervidly (your spouse is under no obligation to thank me). Love every day that is given to you, especially if you are given that day with someone else. I pray that I will never forget the feeling of real love, as I feel it has to be one of the best gifts I have ever been privileged to be given.

**Oh yeah? Who's the only one here who knows secret Ninja moves from the government?**

...I don't know if it has always been a streak of bad luck, but I really don't go to the movies often. Jason and I were always NOTORIOUS for picking the worst movie, spending the small ransom, and walking out saying, "...well, there's 134 minutes of your life you'll never get back..." One word, *Powder*. So for me I've never understood people who go to the movies, because to me (and my lack of good choices) it's always seemed like a waste...hit the Red Box and get comfortable...

There are a few movies from my childhood
that my kids would never be able to
experience in the theater, and thanks to ABC
Family, we DVRed enough of them for a
while. The pinnacle of these was one we
watched on New Year's Day, *the Goonies*.
For me the big appeal, when I was the
'Talls' age, was Sean Astin...convinced that
someday we would get married. I'd watched
every episode of the *Patty Duke Show*, it
was as if I knew his mom already...so very
delusional, and only 10...

Watching it with them, I was convinced that
this perhaps was one of the 'must' movies of
my childhood. Then lost some street cred
with the boys as Jason and I stole A LOT of
quotes from that movie over the years. The
fellas would hear one, and then suddenly
shoot a look to me, as if perhaps I coined the
phrase and THEY were borrowing it. Then,
they got wise.

As we walked out of getting our picture
taken for our church directory this week, I
was struck with a character from a movie
that is watched rather regularly around here,
*Napoleon Dynamite*. The photographer tried
to take a couple of 'glamor' shots of me,
gross. Clearly I have enough pictures of
myself with my hand under my chin. While

walking to the car I said to the Talls, "I felt like I was at 'Glamor Shots by Deb' just now..." To which, without missing a beat they said, "...is there some kind of vest that I can wear?" Jason would have been laughing...

The one of the favorites around here, besides the mandatory Rankin-Bass holiday favorites and other holiday movies, was *Nanny McPhee* and its part two. At first I thought it was because the boys (who by their own right, should work on the publishing of IMDB someday as they are fascinated at basically nothing) were busy finding characters from the Harry Potter series in these movies. Then we watched them, and watched them...and then it got me thinking...

I know why people spend hundreds of dollars a year going to movies...THE ESCAPE of a darkened room, sticky floor, and the blasting sound of a movie to transport you. The place it takes you is somewhere better, if for only 134 minutes. I get it. I'd still rather do it in my pajamas and on my own couch, but I get it.

But there is only so much of a bewitching nanny that makes you start to wonder as a mother...IS THIS A HINT? IS THIS AN ESCAPE, OR IS ART IMITATING LIFE? It did seem rather more than ironic that our lives slightly resembled that of what we were watching on a tri-weekly basis. Maybe my kids need to believe in this fictional nanny, hope for such a magically sacred woman to come to the door and 'fix' life? I found myself wishing it were real too, and I took the hint! I made a call. While she's not magical or bewitching, at least I don't think so? We ought to have something in the works in the next couple of weeks for a 'fix' on things for now...if not, I'll always have my "Glamor Shot by Deb"...

**...the need for adult conversation...**

Well...today was one of those 'well' days. If I were reading about this day I'd say, "Well, so far so good, keep your chin up..." But talking to yourself with four kids in toe sort of doesn't bode well for mental sanity, so I try to keep a lid on it. When possible...unless

I'm at Wal-Mart, and then it's just to keep my cart from running people over.

After two months, how do I feel? If someone were to ask me that, they probably would think I'm deranged, as the answer would teeter this way and that. There are certain variables that I feel I cannot avoid, just have to 'walk through' them. But I'll be honest, it would be a lot more fun to 'walk through' with a cocktail in my hand and an adult to talk to. The phrase 'walk through' is a coined grief phrase, and sadly it's true. You want to run, sprint, skip, hell I'd walk on my hands if I thought I could somehow make the process faster/easier/painless, but it just can't be.

Four months ago, if you asked me if I could handle four kids on my own I would have fallen down on the floor laughing, stating something along the lines of , "...are you fragging NUTS?!" But here I am. It was brought to my attention from my bestie's mom, that at times there is a bit of a double standard when losing a spouse. If a man loses his wife with four kids to raise, it's not an unusual thought that he would HAVE to have someone move in to help him. If a woman loses her spouse with said kids, there are offers for help (to which she appreciates

more than coffee and booze) but she is sort
of expected to go it alone. Figure it out.
Make it work. Now, don't get me wrong,
mentioning this is in no way a ploy
to attempt to gain sympathy. In fact, for me
it is sort of like a badge of courage, albeit a
lonely, starved for adult conversation, sleep
deprived badge of courage...I'll take it.

But then there are the reminders. The times
of day when you are run down and you don't
have 5 o'clock to look forward to. Or there
are days when looking at pictures, I don't
mean albums, I mean just the ones that are
on your walls, are too much to handle. You
sort of feel like a rat in a maze. Then you
feel guilty for feeling that way because,
well, let's face it, these are your rats and this
is your maze. You are mainly trying to work
the clock. Work the clock so everyone gets
fed, takes a nap, has clean clothes, brushes
their teeth, changes their underwear, then
fed again, feels loved, cleaning a fish bowl,
has special time, is nurtured, then eating
again, learning a chore (if only they could
cook), books read, prayers said, and kissed
goodnight...In all this time of working the
clock, I'm begged to ask the question, when
did we have fun?

While I miss Jason, I anguish at the notion, when are we going to have fun again? I miss it, like we can't get it started...it seems like it was much easier to do with Jason in our lives. It also seems we are going to have to really WORK IT to have it happen around here. Try to be spontaneous, but work it all the same. So, with that notion, that was my plan today...and it sort of worked.

We headed to Quincy, EARLY so that we could go to church, go out for breakfast and do a little shopping. I was dreading going to our old church as the last time I was there wasn't a day I wanted to relive. Oscar had an excellent idea to sit somewhere different than we used to, and we did. I sat there, wrestling Atticus, looking at this BEAUTIFUL church. My mind racing to all the wonderful things that happened there, my wedding, the kid's baptisms. But it was my last visit there that is more prominent on my heart, saying goodbye to Jason. I felt like I held it together, we lived to tell the tale and went on to the next part of our journey...breakfast.

I don't know why I even bother shopping for anything other than breakfast items, my kids would eat it constantly! We headed to The Village Inn, and though it was crowded, we got right in, a Sunday miracle! We sat down...and out of nowhere...we started to have fun...all of us. It dawned on me that it was also the first time since Jason passed that I had taken ALL of the kids out to eat, and we were surviving it...and Nora was serenading us, as expected.

Here's my SHOUT-OUT to the wait staff at The Village Inn, you are awesome. Stacey, I'm mainly talking to you. I was so overwhelmed at how nice/helpful/kind she was to us that I left her a large tip. I asked the manager if I could have a number to give them a recommendation. We nearly made it...until the manager wanted to give me his LIFE STORY as my four kids sat unattended at a table (thus far they'd been angels, it's the law of averages really). I turn around when I hear Oscar loudly **say**, "ATTI!" I turn around and the little grubber has grasped the syrup bottle and is getting ready to make-it-rain-syrup! Praise the Lord, some woman sitting across from us got up and took the bottle out of his hand, greeted me as I came running over and complimented me. I was on cloud nine... not only had I survived it, we had fun, and I did it alone, nearly.

...I almost made it out, when the waitress came over to thank me for her tip. I told her, "It's <u>you</u> I have to thank, this is the first time I've been brave enough to take all my kids out alone...and we had fun!" Of course I got teary, hugged her, and told her our story. I figured I had the tears coming since I didn't let loose earlier.

The last two months have seemed like a year. It's still hard to wrap my brain around our new life. I wonder when normal will no longer be something I think about. At times I feel like I didn't really ask for a 'dare-to-be-great-situation', that was someone else...I don't need to have some sob story of a life that is somehow played on the Hallmark Channel...I just want to try to survive the maze, raise the rats, and have some fun again.

### ...table of hell, party of 5?

...well, never let it be said too often how very much I love living where I do. This little gem of a town that has taken us in, and taken care of us. Every day I wake up and love this house more. While it was supposed to be OUR dream, I feel like it still is, just readjusted...

At any given moment, I live in a **'state of terror'** when it comes to going anywhere with four kids. If you see me out in public and it looks like I-have-it-together, it's only because as you look away one of my kids is setting Walmart on fire. This **'state of terror'** has to be dealt with at times or I'd never leave my house. So, you go at it head on, but lock yourself in the bathroom before you leave and give yourself a good pep-talk...praying you make it out, back, and in one piece with no one visibly limping.

This town has no clubs to speak of, no women's groups that I have found per say, just "get-togethers" as I was told early on. I couldn't help not knowing that, as everyone I ran across said they had been to a Christmas party in my house before I lived there. While this Christmas we weren't really in the party mood, I thought, maybe next year we would. I'm so very lucky that my neighbors and I are all roughly the same age group, have kids, know/need to have a good time! We meet out in the empty lot on a nice day, our kids screaming like banshees, swap parenting stories, perhaps open the beer fridge and just catch up. These people in the last 5+ months have seen/been through a lot with me, and I am forever grateful for them. Whether it's to have another parent to talk to, home repair question to ask, or just someone to laugh with. These people have been brought into my life, and I am a blessed person because of it.

So, the neighbors invited us to a dinner party...cut to me, 15 minutes before we leave, in the bathroom giving myself a pep talk. Praying my cranky baby can pull it together, my sleep deprived 3 year old can muster some charm, and my ROWDY BOYS can dial it back enough not to destroy someone else's home just so Mom can talk to an adult. At this point if my hair were long enough I'd be chewing on it...

Going, even down the street, with four kids stresses me out, and I seriously have to get over it! My kids haven't spent time in Juvie? My kids know how to be polite...my kids can mingle with the best of them, right? Well, I felt horrible, we need to learn how to be fashionably late for once. No, we're the nerds who get to the party THE MINUTE IT STARTS. I was praying the whole time that my kids would just go upstairs, any carnage that might have taken place wouldn't be seen by other adult non-kid-bringers. Nora was the first back down stairs. Never to let a cocktail table go un-noticed, she sat down directly in front of the cookies, where I told her she needed to have one cookie and then something else, preferably healthy. I told her she should introduce herself to the adult next to her, she did. To which an adult asked her if she would like a carrot and she said, "You know, I don't mind if I do..."

The house started to fill with people. The 'adult drinks' were pointed out, to those who wished to partake. You could just feel the fun...the buzz of the kids up stairs...the chatting of the people there. These neighbors need to open their home for Christmas tours, un-be-lieve-able! I was in awe! I was also in awe that none of my children demolished a tree while we were there! While I dreaded going, not because I didn't think I would have fun, I just dread going anywhere without my adult sidekick and all of these FRAGGIN' kids. I've tried to put into better terms how it is to go to a party when you are in my situation...I've decided that it is much akin to walking in somewhere topless, or with half of your pants on. It's sort of uncomfortable, but really only for you...so you just get over it, eventually.

So, here I am, mentally topless, and it was...fun. It was fun to let my kids play (I'm very sorry that they possibly tore up your house). It was fun to meet new people, laugh and see these cherished beings I am thankful to call neighbors. It was so very fun to witness what I'd been hearing about, the 'get-togethers'!

But as all good things must come to an end, Nora came up to me, and gave me a look that I knew all too well. I told her to go tell her brothers it was time to go. I put Atticus' coat on him, walked through the dining room and said, "Well, it's all fun until someone wets their pants, and thank God it wasn't me..."

**...get yourself one!**

...I am a woman. Plain and simple. We are full of drama, insecurities, and tiniest bit of self-loathing, all because we are women...that is, unless you have a good man by your side...a person who can completely squash all of those would-be-negative-thoughts, just by telling you...you are beautiful.

I have had a man like that...someone who you see a picture of and think (still to this day), smoking' hot. A man that knows you so well that he can not only finish your sentences, but knows better than to contemplate the question you may ask him, "How do I look?" A man that is willing to have a good time with you no matter how pregnant you are. A man that is able to see the flaws in you, and build you up so that the flaws are something wonderful. A man that can shoot you a look from across a room and you might possibly blush, because you know what he is thinking. A man that isn't afraid of buying maxi-pads, girlie razors, or lotion, because he knows he is man enough. A man that despite it all, can always make you feel beautiful, even though you don't really believe it.

Like I said, I have had this man, and while I feel like I might have never deserved him, I feel like somehow he has never left. I look in the mirror, and despite of the way I might have felt two seconds prior, I feel/hear him in my head, building me up. I hear him say something totally inappropriate in my head when Atticus, in a rowdy temper tantrum, pulls down my pajama bottoms in the kitchen. I hear him ranting about government, disgusted with reality TV...Laughing when my Nora delivers an inappropriate, "You GOT TO BE FREAKIN' KIDDING ME?!" with just the right inflection. Cheering when Atticus takes a few scant steps. Or cracking up that within 8 seconds of the credits of *The Karate Kid*, everyone started doing the 'crane'...

I feel like I need these things to all happen, feelings to come about, to really know how very wonderful a man I had...and how I sort of miss blushing at something inappropriate!

**...the thank you that Hallmark can't send bourbon with...**

I turned on my computer, slightly curious. My friend April just downloaded some long overdue items to my computer this weekend. While I knew what it was, I didn't dare look/listen to it until I was alone. I'm no dummy, at this point I can see the waves coming from hundreds of feet out...it all just depends on my endurance as to if I can jump them or get plowed over, bringing me to my figurative knees, leaving me sort of shaken, wondering if I will recover or whether I should just let go and float.

I have sort of adopted this secret life after 8pm. Now, don't get me wrong, it's not exciting, thrilling, or even probably worth mentioning, it's just quiet TV/computer/writing time...basically an unknown sort of rut, but seriously, look at my daily life, I'm excited by very little. But, this weekend was different...I had an adult to talk to for FOUR WHOLE DAYS!!!

First, I need to thank my brother for his thoughtfulness of adding my best friend of nearly 20 years to his 'buddy pass' plan on American Airlines. With this she can pass fly here 12 times in the next year any time she wants. Thank you to Joel Van Gilder. It is truly an immeasurable gift and I will be forever indebted to you...the gift of an old friend that can take you away without having to even leave, that was my weekend, and that was just the beginning...

Then there is this friend of 20 years, who seriously I feel like, as the events in my life unveil, we met certainly by no accident. April Hershey Lovegrove, thank you for taking off work, coming to this madhouse I call a home, never getting to sleep in, having cocktails with me, talking/ listening, giggling with me/crying with me until the wee hours of the night, and treating my kids like they are your own. You are someone I thank God for knowing, let alone being my friend, every day. You have always been special to me, but to see that feeling exude from my children is something that not only makes my heart smile, but I feel like Jason is smiling too. You took me out of my rut for 4 days, and I miss you already! Can't wait for March!

Then there is a special thank you to these other group of friends, which thanks to social media I can keep up with them and them me even if we haven't seen each other in years. The gift you have given my children, so that they can have lasting memories of their father, well, is nothing short of amazing. The thoughtfulness and kindness you have shown my children have reinforced my belief in paying it forward. If I teach them nothing else in this life of mine, I will teach them that in your name. My family and I are blessed to know you, thank you from the bottom of our hearts.

So, there I was...in the quiet of 7:45 pm...First I turned on his music...all the while hearing him say, "Now, don't fast forward through to the songs you like, listen to the whole damn thing and get the feel for it!" I started to smile. I thought to myself, now time to look at the video. I haven't watched it since shortly after his funeral. At first I was just marveling...Seeing, mainly hearing, but seeing my kids every day, I miss their little features, that are so very their father. In looking at the pictures of Jason as a child, I could see glimpses of him in every single one of my children. Things I had never noticed before…it made me smile. But in the distance I could see it. In the distance I could see a wave, wondering if it would spare me.

Then the pictures of Jason came on from our life together...I didn't jump in time, figuratively and literally I was taken out at the knees, giving up the fight and decided to float...knowing that it was inevitable. So, tonight all I can say is that no matter what wave of emotion I might be riding at any given time, no matter if I surmount it or decided to float... I am grateful for friends, family, and knowing what the other side of the rut looks like...bring on March!

## ...wanted: adult conversations without fart jokes...

...so, I'm to that point...somewhere between anger, alienation, and anguish. There are no postcards here, no t-shirts for sale, and the view pretty much sucks. For every ten feet we get as a family, I feel like it is sort of a beard for me...and sometimes the beard falls off at the very worst times...

All the clichés apply here...four kids, little to no free time, feeling as though I send my kids to bed not because it's always time, but because I am emotionally/mentally spent. The last week I have tried to PACK my life with stuff to do, to just get my focus on anything but my actual thoughts.

Thankfully, my kids have helped me in this by trying to find things that WE can do together, maybe the postcards suck where they are too. Lego night was fun, and cocktail food for dinner, well, pretty much rocks, but something is still missing...

I never knew how important adult conversation was, until I had to phone it in to get it. I love my children, but sometimes I need adults to talk to...contemplated, wouldn't it be great to have a sitter come over and talk to ME?I rethought that, I don't want to fall into that demographic, yet.

I feel like I'm saying the same things over and over...I feel like I want to get out into the world, but then 'chicken' out for the sake of calling a sitter for my kids. I feel like something just isn't right, and I cannot fix it, and it's IRRITATING. All the while, I'm lost in this little 'pity-party-world' and all these amazing things are going on around me...

We got a piano! Now, while I am grateful, I was seriously hoping to find a teacher by now, the rambunctious banging on this poor piano, always followed by Nora yelling, "**I did it, I played *Jingle Bells!!!*"**...it's starting to make me worried that no teacher will want us! As well as her interest in drumming with pencils, being a bag lady, construction worker, doctor, and always wanting to be called handsome instead of beautiful...I've stopped trying to figure that one out.

The boys are full on into Legos, iPad, reading, video games, having smelly feet, telling gross jokes, farting (and always laughing at it), kick boxing (sport of the future and no training), and subliminally needing **spring to get here so they can run off some major steam**! They are also taking

a new interest in their young sapling of a
brother, running him as ragged as they can,
and despite the above mentioned I am
grateful.

Then there is this little sprite of a person,
growing, and acquiring all this personality
seemingly all at once. Atticus will be a year
old in two weeks and he is a spit fire! He's
started walking, and is getting pretty good at
it. I caught him today, yelling at Nora
through the bathroom door, all the while
making faces in the mirror, watching
himself and then cracking up. He gets into
EVERYTHING at a speed that would baffle
an engineer. All of these things are
happening, and I'm the only one seeing it.
I'm the only one marveling at it...and well at
times while I should be so grateful, I find
myself feeling really alone...and then
worrying that they are feeling the same way.
Then there are the weird things that
happen...chest hair.

 Now Jason, due to the meds he was on,
never lacked chest hair, or arm hair, or any
other place that one could get hair. Through
the years I stopped noticing the vast
amounts of hair that was around our
house...but lately, out of the clear blue

nowhere, I will find a chest hair...just one...and in weird places around the house.

Now, I realize I am grasping at straws here, but when I find them they sort of crack me up and make me stop and think...and then sort of miss my hairy friend, husband, and conversationalist. The person who knew all my stories and teammate in this game of life...then it's off to find a new beard, to hopefully hide behind for a little while...

**...glass slippers and severed legs...**

…frazzled…running…scurrying…hiding…busy work…callowness...currently, this is the location I am stuck in, or rather the place I have settled myself. I'm not sure why?...maybe it is easier to ignore my real life, my real feelings, or even time for just me...and while I thought it was a fun 'Band-Aid' to my daily life, at times it can be a lot more work mentally than I am capable of...

It's a gift to talk to someone, and say anything. It's a gift, especially right now, to not have to mentally judge where someone 'thinks' you need to be in your head...to speak freely, not worried if you will come off too happy, too sad, or just down right inappropriate. At the same time it's sort of like riding in the carriage that you know will turn into a pumpkin at midnight. It's a thrill, but you know real life still awaits you, and there are toilets to clean (boys are gross, and if I could pee standing up, you know that aim would be the first thing I would master)...dishes, laundry, butts to wipe and tantrums to endure...I'm not looking to wear the glass slipper, just wanting a little time to escape...yet, it's bitter sweet.

I have learned, that I have a lot to learn about life and people. There are people out there who seem to only exist to take on a cause, at times in spite of their relationship with that cause. Who would have ever thought that there are people out there, who actually burgeon on some one's loss or pain? There are also people out there who enjoy conjuring up people's pain, to wear as THEIR badge of honor. While these people, excuse me, piss me off...fact of the matter is, if these people have to peddle your loss, pain, struggle, not only are they not friends, their lives must be lacking contentment. For that I guess I have to pity them, like I haven't got enough to do...

I say this, and feel like somehow these 'cause heads' have made me stronger, besides what I've already gone through. I don't know if I had the confidence 3 months ago that I have today...it's sort of a quiet exhilaration. Like I climbed Everest, and didn't even pack a backpack, I'm that bad-ass...don't get me wrong, I'm not stuck on myself, but I feel like I've faced more than a few fears lately. I can honestly say, while it scares the crap out of me, inevitably there will be more, and I'm ready.

Then there is the instance where the neighbor kid gets caught in your Murphy Bed...and while you aren't proud of a few of the words you uttered, terrified as you were imagining that perhaps they had severed a leg, I mean really!? The next day you have to laugh at the notion of how in the world it all happened in the first place...it's not Everest, but definitely, lesson learned.

I, while I am not proud of this, have become fairly intolerant to people's 'problems'. I understand and fully accept people's feelings (grief, pain, fear, etc.) you can't help the feelings you have, otherwise you wouldn't have them, and by that right you are entitled to them. I'm talking about those 'problems' that people have, that are brought onto themselves...over scheduling, over extending, the self-induced chaos sort of stuff...all the while as I listen to them list all of the things that they are dealing with. I mentally fix myself a cocktail, and think, "You, ARE RIGHT that must be tough considering you have a spouse to fall back on when necessary...poor, thing". My 'sister' Gail has told me that I have a 'bitch card' that I am able to use freely for the next 2 years...I have, at times, had my hand in my pocket, secretly holding this card, teetering on the edge of using it...I've yet to whip it out.

...I don't write my thoughts down for pity, concern, sympathy or attention...I write them because I need to get it either out of my head, off my mind, or just simply to release it from my soul. I don't claim to have all the answers, be the best mother, or even a decent human being...I am flawed, have issues, and while I know that these are what make up my being, I'm not always proud of them. But I own them, because they are me. Although, if you see my hands in my pockets, you have been warned...

**...hey, this one is for you...**

...so, somehow, for whatever reason...I don't
say this enough, I am thankful...
It's not that I had to go through something
difficult to know what I had already...it's not
like losing one part of my life made me
think any clearer...or being freaked out made
me blinded to the world around me...I
always knew you were there, I just sort of
forgot for a moment...

Maybe I had just temporarily put you on the
back burner. Maybe I remembered all the
silly things we did way back when, but
figured I'm OLD AS CRAP now and that
was then. Perhaps I always remembered the
fun we had at times and needed a wakeup
call that those memories don't have to be in
the past because we are now slightly grey
haired underneath it all. Those recollections
of the times once were with you, the ones
that make me smile and laugh...

So if we giggled at a slumber party,
swapped stories in a foreign land, drank
together in college, worked together with the
elderly...the nurses who saw right-down-my-
main-street for my babies (and still call me a
friend), the mothers who I was lucky enough
to meet and swap stories/laughs with, the

people who have checked in on me because of Jason, and those who have recently taken my slightly fragile family and I under their wing...

Lately, all these above mentioned people I have been blessed to somehow have in my life, are what have gotten me through. I've audibly heard my self saying, "I am the luckiest person alive to have friends like this..." Thank you from the bottom of my heart, you will never know how very special you are and the strength you give me...

## ...17, slightly naive and fences...

...so it dawned on me today, as I was telling the same story to two different people...seemingly, as if I were saying, "...and then I took out the trash..." I have a past... (Cue creepy orchestra music). As telling all the tales of my sorted life could get me in trouble, possibly arrested, or never spoken to again, I will stick with one story of my youth...when I was 17...

I traveled to Germany to be an exchange student for a year. Before we were sent off into a foreign land, they taught us a little German, let us drink a little, and wished us well. Quickly, I learned that there should have been a few other refresher courses offered, such as "Child Labor and the American".

Now, I should have known from the first letter, before I even flew over the ocean, that these people were slightly unorthodox...I still remember my brother looking at a few pictures the German family whom I would be living with sent. I believe his direct quote was, "...well, it looks like they lay out topless with their dog there, good luck..." I tried/hoped/prayed that this was just some cultural thing that we weren't used to...it was only the beginning.

I get to these people's house, knowing very little German, them knowing even less English and thought, okay lady, sink or swim. But as time went on, I realized they were not hosting a student for cultural enlightenment, they had a business scheme. I would do all of the foot work and they would collect the money. As the days turned to weeks, and I noticed that while there are 'cultural differences' there are also no words to describe your German dad walking in on you in the bathroom, EVERY TIME YOU ARE IN IT, clothed or unclothed. Old German Grandpas grabbing your behind, not being fed, never being able to clean your clothes...I quickly started picking up German, but decided I ought to play dumb as while I was around them I could be entertained by the fact that they spoke about me in German...

Only as an adult did I understand why they always had me make calls on Sundays. They would drive me to one of their works, arm me with a flashlight and point to a phone. Thankfully, I made a call that would change my life. Terrified that I was just being un-adaptable, I called the first name I saw on the list. I was instructed I had five minutes, and in those five minutes I managed to say Happy Birthday, and ask as many questions as possible, "...does your host dad try to watch you bathe? Do you get fed? Are you working?"

Thankfully, someone tipped off the Exchange Program I was with that these people's intentions weren't correct...I would be moved to another family. Well, to say that ruffled some German feathers...The day I was supposed to leave, they locked me out of the house, and told me the only way I was going to get my things was to climb their back gate and get it myself. Me, 5 foot something? And I don't know if you know this, but GERMAN SHEPHERDS are like the number one dog in Germany...I vaguely ever saw this dog, just heard him and he sounded like KUJO. Cut to me, scaling an 8 foot fence, gently whispering, "Good doggie...nice doggie...", and running like hell to the back door to get my suitcase! This wild story ends here, from this point comes one of a family that took me in, taught me about their culture, and treated me like family, and still to this day I am blessed to have them in my life.

Now, I sit and laugh at the absurdity of the whole thing, and sort of marvel at the fact that I made it out with one of my very best friends, a billion more stories, and a group of then teenagers who knew me when (and I seriously consider them family today)...I'm grateful for the experience, beyond thankful for the stories, and gratified by the notion that I might have a past...

## ...three months down...

...three months ago today...I was hopeful and terrified...I was wide-eyed and scared...I was intentionally ignorant at the notion that he would not be coming home...mainly because I just couldn't think about my life, my kids, my heart having to function without him...he would rally, he would have limitations, and while that would have crushed him mentally, I would still have him...frail but fierce...but that didn't happen...

At first he was everywhere, I couldn't take a shower without thinking of him, struggling to breathe the last time he was in it...I would look at his open closet door and it was too much...Just looking at a picture would slightly send me into tears...but honestly, I didn't have time/desire/or the strength to break down...I didn't WANT to break down in front of our kids. I didn't want them to have to associate memories of him and feel sad. He can be a part of our lives without having to be sad, the best memories are the ones that make you smile deep within you, and work their way to your face...

So, unsure of how I would do it, I had to tackle life without my very best friend. Slowly I began to feel him giving me strength and confidence, patience and presence of mind, and the ability to look at his pictures and smile, usually uttering as I walked away, "...smokin' hot..."-that was him. I feel like now more than ever before I can see why people are brought into your life years before you have to deal with a tragedy, they were meant to help you deal...and you just thought you liked them because they were cool...COSMICALLY COOL!!

I also am beginning to see the 'forest for the trees' on life. If you try to stare at any one aspect, dwell on all of the things you are missing from your life, your heart or your world, or worry when/where/how you will feel better, you will eventually miss out on the little things that can go on around you. The milestones that you can celebrate in spite of how you feel, the events that can help you heal...

So three months later, I am still thanking him. Thanking him for being so good to me, leaving me these blessings of children and being able to see him in all of them. Thanking him for helping me remember that a sense of humor about life keeps you out of the liquor cabinet...and secretly giving me more strength than I ever knew I was capable of having. Despite not having what I want, I have what I need and require to go on frail but fierce...


**...February babies...**

...it's coming up on two years soon. Every woman has a 'labor story' to tell, and they should. It's their badge of honor, their hour (let's face it usually more than one) of glory...however, this one is different...this one starts with the sad ending, and ends with on remarkable story...

At my nineteen week ultra sound, I went in to the little room, nervous if I was having a boy or a girl... chatting nonstop, mainly trying to talk Jason into finding out what we were having. Then the ultrasound nurse became very quiet, and the room became heavy, soon after so did our hearts. The baby had died, and now I was going to have to go to the hospital to deliver it...

When you have 3 kids, going to the labor and delivery floor is also a badge of honor, but this time was clearly different.

Thankfully I had an angel of a friend (who is also a nurse) and she put the word out to her friends working, about me. This nurse came in, Jason and I were both taking turns crying. The nurse said, "I'm Jamie, I'm friends with Shannon, and I'm going to take care of you..." Dozens of hours later, life was very different, Jamie totally understood what we were going through, took such good care of us, even offering to stay over her shift to help. She was this unbelievable person, who I had never met, she was our angel...

Fast forward, 10 or 15 months, we found out again, we were pregnant...and to think they told us we'd never get pregnant...and clearly we should be taking up another hobby, but anyway. I find out my angel of a nurse, Jamie, is also pregnant! We exchange clothes for babies, she is having her first girl, and me a boy...what are the odds? It's February 12th, I am feeling major contractions, still 10 days out from my due date, my doctor said to go ahead and head up to the maternity floor, get checked in and we'll see what's up. I get into the room to find, Jamie! This adorable little gal who is CLEARLY as pregnant as I am! We started chatting about how she was feeling, how she too was some days away from her due date.

She gets me hooked up to the equipment and the waiting game starts...

About five hours later, when she comes in, I notice she's sort of walking differently than she had before. She checks what she needs to check, and then turns to me and says, "...well, I hate to tell you this, but I am in the process of getting you another nurse, my contractions are running 5 minutes apart and I am getting ready to head next door and get in a bed..." I was like, WHAT? What are you doing here? Get over there girl!
It's like the most wonderful gift, to be shared by a common story that is anything but common. This woman who not only took care of me with her knowledge and her hands, but also her heart. I really felt blessed have my last child share a birthday with what was bound to be an amazing girl, it's in her genes you know...A few hours later, Atticus was born, on February 12, 2012...he now has this link, a forever friend, born an hour later, Avery...this little girl, with 3 brothers, the forever princess!

Why am I telling this story? Because there are people who are brought into your life for reasons unknown to you....because before you are aware of it, you have connections to people who you have never met...because

this is my last 'labor story' and I'm so very
lucky to share it with this angel of a nurse,
who helped me at such a dark time, only to
now celebrate the reason for our
connection...our February babies...

## Bad moods and cupcakes...who knew?

...I try to bury it. I try to push it to the
deepest part of my brain...but it sifts its way
up every once and a while. Although, I
know I shouldn't whine, I know I shouldn't
be angry, as I know it does nothing to help
my situation. Never-the-less I am in a rut
that I feared I'd be in someday, and well,
today is the day...

A bad mood? Yeah, that comes close to
summing it up...I guess it is a mixture of
mood, exhaustion, and never seeing an end
to being out numbered...never seeing an end
to a 'Band-Aid' on whatever is going on.
Knowing that a manicure, haircut, coffee,
and I can't believe I am saying this, even a
cocktail isn't going to help this. Sadly, night

falls and morning rises and the whole thing starts again...Thankfully, I am not in this mood all the time, I'd say so far it's even been rare, but today...today is something different...Today is a mixture of regret, fear, and knowing that there will be at least four more times I will feel like this in the next calendar year...

Tomorrow, we will be celebrating Atticus's 1st birthday, and I want sort of nothing to do with it, how horrible is that? All the other's first birthdays were parties or celebrations, and today I have no desire to celebrate-insert mother guilt here, and wow, does it sting! It's ridiculous to think, had someone told me a year ago where I'd be today, I would have spit in their face...but, it is where I am...and for the first time (seriously), I want to pack it all in and run away. Surely, running away will take this mood away? Going somewhere so far from my daily life will take my mind to a better place? Knowing that I have to pull it together, even if I don't want to do any of it? There isn't a solution.

While I've prided myself on pushing through the crap, hitting it head on, and wearing some imaginary 'badge'...it still doesn't take away from the fact that today, I am overwhelmed...with thoughts, workload, talking children, and wishing I weren't doing this alone...wishing I didn't have to be strong...wishing...

Bad moods are just par for the course and I need to quit my whining, hit it head on, and have a cocktail later...I can't possibly bring back what is missing...I also have no desire to try...it just delays the inevitable...maybe that's where my bad mood has settled, and for now it can bite it.

## The Sisters Anita and Lydia would be proud...

...so, like any good parent, this morning I approached the subject of Lent with my kids...discussing what it is all about and why we as Catholics do it. I was trying to get some concrete notion to them that they were old enough to 'give up' something but also they could start a new 'habit' that could possibly better themselves over the next 40 days. The Talls standard Lenten sacrifice is Legos, so it was no surprise when they mentioned that, Nora saying she was,

"...giving up men" however, was interesting, but we'll get back to her.

As a child, I always gave up candy...pretty standard, however in hindsight, it seems rather for not, as Easter was always some gluttonous candy extravaganza. So, I guess I was just saving up some diabetic shock for Easter day? What did I learn from it? Did I forever abandon what I gave up after Easter? Not usually...In examining my life the past 3+ months, I was thinking of all the things I could give up, and then realized, those few things are the ones that get me through to the next day. For that matter, I feel like I've given up quite a few things in those same 3 months, what now (she says with yellow eyes and slightly drooling)?

Lent doesn't have to be a dreaded four-letter-word, why can't it be a time to better yourself, life, or situation? Oddly enough, I decided early this morning that while I could be annoyed about giving something up, I could actually learn something from paying attention to life around me...little did I know what kind of fodder it would be giving me.

Atticus, while creeping around, EVERYWHERE, is slightly a laugh a minute. He sort of maneuvers like an 80 year old, every once and a while his feet move faster than his body. He talks, loudly, non-stop and sort of looks at you like, "...come on you dolt, what part of what I just said didn't you get?!" Then just walks away talking to himself. He knows all the trademark baby stuff; peek-a-boo, waving, clapping...but tonight he invented a new game, the Kiss-Attack. I'm not sure how it started, but he just kept coming at me mouth open trying to kiss me, and laughing his pants off...it's a cute, slightly juicy game, that I hope wears off before he's 12...

The boys, a.k.a. Talls, well, they are starting to get to that age. Alone, they wouldn't be there yet, but together, it's like they are some sort of gross super-duo. Like they combined their age to make a teenager (I say this, although I know they are good kids, but let's face it, the boys out number me in this house). They are starting to notice certain things. At first I thought it was my imagination, but then tonight, when they were thumping around (what is it with boys and stomping everywhere?! I mean good God they'd wake the dead!). We finally moved their calendar up to February on their Star Wars Calendar...and I was smacked in the face with what I thought I might have possibly been noticing. There she was,

Princess Leah, in the "Golden Bikini". I saw Oscar's eyes sort of change, as he seemingly couldn't move his eyes away. Then without thinking, and let's face it, forgetting I was there, he said rather quickly to Abe, "...Abe, do you see that....?" I decided my best move was to simply walk out of the room. Anything I could have added would have scared or muddle them up for life. Like they always say, first it's the Golden Bikini, then...

Now, I shouldn't always leave Nora for last, but let's face it...she's the one who speaks to me THE MOST during the day. If I had to catalog all the bat-shit-crazy things she said, this thing would be as long as _Gone With The Wind_. I do find it interesting the things she does pick up on, and how she speaks freely, without any worry of how it might sound, or if it is even right. If she doesn't know, it doesn't stop her from speaking, she just starts making up words to fit what she is saying. Tonight, however ended like most nights, her still talking straight until I say, "...goodnight, I love you…". However, the content was, well, Nora. Tonight, she was telling me that she'd like to listen to Harry Connick Jr. to go to sleep. As I was getting the cd out, I mentioned how he looked pretty dreamy on the cover, to which she says, "I know, when I hear him singing, I just end up dreaming about him, and we talk and talk..." Then when I gave her a kiss goodnight she said, "...well, that was an extra juicy..."

...this is the stuff I need to pay attention to...this is the stuff that will make a crap day better...this is the stuff that you will grow from knowing about your kids, because for one moment you paid attention and maybe got a laugh...this is what I am doing for Lent, and I hope by doing it, it's a habit I can always keep.

## ...when is it time to know?

...dealing with all that goes along with 4 kids: orthodontic head gear, teething, bed wetting, hormonal out bursts (theirs and mine), emotional moments, laundry, meals, shopping, snack lists, school work, and the 12 hours of questions every day, such as, "Why can't Sunny (a stuffed animal) just pee where ever he wants?"-to which I still don't have a sufficient enough answer for her. It is easy to get lost...actually more like devoured by life...but after it all goes to bed for the day, or in the moments when I am actually alone (there are some, not enough, but there are), I'm left with a question...

In the last 17 years I have been some one's girlfriend, some one's fiancé, some one's wife, some one's mother...that's a lot wrapped up all into one. Any mother knows, at some point you sort of lose yourself after having children; your waistline, your sleep, your wardrobe, your spontaneity, your identity, your drive...that being said, you lose these things because you are a good mother. The same can be said after getting married, if you are lucky enough, you lose these things yet it doesn't matter to your spouse, because you have each other...you are the yin to their yang...but what happens when you lose your yang?

In all the crazy that is my day, I downplay most of what others comment on, as this is my life...the fact that it is stressful, slightly endless at times, doesn't give me the right to glean any sort of prize other than the fact that I can't run away from it. I can't clock-out and drive away to a quieter, easier life...this is where I live. While at times it's difficult, I have to embrace the madness and dish out the ice cream...but there is something lying underneath it all. Something that is very difficult to grapple, as I haven't had to before. While one of my job descriptions is still valid on my resume, there is another that isn't, and it has me sort of lost for words (yeah, now is the time I'm lost for words, write that one down folks!)...

I'm only 37, and even though I spent my last birthday thinking I was turning 36, I still feel like I am young...until I do the emotional math of where I have resided in the last 3 months. While I feel like it ages me about 15 years, there I am still 37 with this story of a life...most of the time lived to the fullest with just a few regrets, as any good life, I feel, should have as you learn from them. I'm 37 and now what? Who am I? Where do I fit in? The whole thing is a creepy mixture of being and adult and in seventh grade all at the same time...but the question weighs heavy on my mind sometimes. I have these talks with a friend going through similar loss, and we both, if given one wish, would fast forward time...I'd fast forward time just to see how things work out. I'd fast forward time to see where my life has taken me...my OCD is in hyper drive at times lately, as I feel like I have control, but just a little, and for about 67 minutes at a time...and no matter how many people say, "Everything will work itself out, just wait you'll see..." doesn't cut it right now. I'm down one job title on my resume. I'm just wondering what to fill it with, when I'll be able to answer all these questions I have in my head, or if I'll ever just be content with **not knowing** an appropriate answer to why 'Sunny' (the stuffed animal) can't pee where ever he wants...

**...mechanical bull Sunday....**

...so, I've already stated I live 'there'...this quaint, quirky, little town. The picture of small town America, the place where everyone knows who you are, the town where people are as nice as they are real, that could fall into any TV show...the people are unique and genuine and it's nestled in anywhere U.S.A. Me? My 'there' is Canton, Missouri- Canton M-O, to those who know me outside of this zip code...

Now, I haven't been officially given the Key to this town yet, but it doesn't really matter...this place is like no other...and the people are one of a kind. Let me just say, I am VERY fortunate, I have been at the right places at the right times before in my life, but now is when I feel I am getting the ultimate payoff. I am so very lucky to have met the people I have in this little town. They not only look out for you, but care enough to check in on you and extend invites to karaoke and mechanical bull afternoons at a local bar- SCORE!

Now, I don't want to get ahead of myself...Canton, MO, is a small town, nestled at the bottom of a hill overlooking the Mississippi River. It is quiet, friendly, and beautiful here, what any great writer writes about when describing a small town...but the people here are an un-tapped treasure! My family and I were invited to a 'family afternoon' at a local bar by more than one resident in the area...At first I thought, well...then one invite included the fact that while there would be kid friendly things/food there, they would also have the adult kind too...I'd be dumb not to go!

Now, my kids aren't really 'bar' savvy, well, what kids are? Anyway, they were astonished as we walked into a bar, I was quick to tell them that 'bar' wasn't a dirty word after all, and we headed to the back...and while the volume increased, so did the fun. My kids were sort of wide eyed, and ecstatic all at the same time. I told them to put their stuff down and get in line to get on that bull! None were brave enough to sing karaoke, but that was enough entertainment in itself.

While there, every kid took one or many turns riding the bull, or if you were Nora, you tried to sweet talk the operator into just letting you JUMP in the protective wall around the bull! These wonderful people took turns taking Atticus, holding him, feeding him, and walking him around the place so that I could not only have an adult conversation, but also feel, well NORMAL! For that, I will be eternally grateful, not to mention looking forward to the next kid-in-the-bar-day!

All this fun, in a bar, in this little town, with these wonderful people, on a mechanical bull, with bar food, soda, loud music, and just random craziness...we got into the van and Oscar said, "...that's probably the most fun I've had in a long while!"...honestly, I couldn't have agreed more!

**...Glamour magazine vs. Thunder Dome...**

...fears...we all have them...some of us HAVE to face them...some of us avoid them, using any excuse imaginable...some people look at them as a challenge and face them head on... Me? Well, I am a mixture of all of these, sort of picking and choosing from a veritable menu of what is convenient at the time...I feel like I've faced some fears, but in the words of Karen Carpenter, "...we've only just begun...". Today, I faced one fear realizing that I'd already been-there-done-that-bought-the-souvenir-cup now writing about it...therapeutic, huh?

The dentist. Up until this morning, I thought I was the only one who feared them...little did I know, there is a bevy of people out there with the same fear. Mine started young, creepy dentist that you'd have to sit in a little room with, alone...now, I'm not saying that I developed schizophrenia from it or anything like that, but it takes one creepy person for me, and then I'm creeped...I now sort of pity dentists, I mean, let's face it, they're shot before they ever walk in the door...

I get to my appointment, early, only to have to wait 35 minutes to be seen...while there I read up on messages, Facebook, and then perused their magazine collection...it still floors me that a *Glamour* magazine could ever be sitting next to *Family Fun* in this universe. As I had no kids looking over my shoulder watching what I was reading, I picked up the *Glamour*. Turns out I learned little that I can actually put into daily use, grateful that I didn't have a child around me who reads, but lessons are lessons...

As I sat there, I sort of became aware of the noise, or lack thereof...at any given moment in my house it sounds like you are sitting front row at THUNDER DOME...I suddenly, figured that even if I had to come back to this office, and see a terrifying (in my head only) dentist, it might be worth it, just for the quiet...I actually thought how nice it would be if I had a blanket and pillow...the quiet actually, calmed me...and here I thought BLARING Beastie Boys did it for me on the drive over...

I think secretly, the biggest fear that I faced today, and one that I might be even more ashamed of admitting, was the fear of doing something for myself...I'm guilty as charged when it comes to hiding behind my children...I was telling someone the other day, these tiny people; whose vast vocabulary, comedic timing, self-aware, are bold, and dimples that you could swim in...these people are my resume, these people are my work...of course, I can go to work in my pajamas, but these are my sales, my checks and balances, my projected blue print of my body of work...to do something, well and let's face it something that cost money, for me, felt weird. Somehow, I've talked myself out of simple things like the dentist, because it didn't add to the 'cause'...

SO, for the next however long, I will be visiting my new 'friend' Doug...thinking less creepy, more quiet, and hoping to score a few back issues of *Glamour*, to catch up on the things I need to know, and wonder if I'll ever get to put them into practice...

**...mind games and the verbal arsenal...**

...so, what is the deal with the time-space-continuum? ...what is an actual measure of time? I mean, I have a calendar, I know the whole thing with counting the days in a month, some have 30, some 31 and so on...but, how is it possible that three and a half months can actually feel like a year? Do I have some cryptic ability? ...am I some bizarre offspring of Nostradamus?

...currently measuring life in minutes seems to best dictate how life rolls here, and not for nothing but 131,040 minutes seems like a long time...

In talking to my bestie (one who reads between my lines), I was reminded of the fact that my initial quest in this new world of mine was to find 'a normal'...little did I anticipate that once found, all of my wildest dreams would not come true...little did I know that finding 'normal' is not only boring, tedious, and monotonous, but also a little lonely...I feel like while my house might not be clean, I don't have all of the doctor appointments caught up, and I need a pedicure...we are all surviving, but to what end? At what point do you just claim mental defeat? ...when do you admit that you might be losing at 'Mental Jenga' (thank you Jennifer Reekie)...

Yesterday, we headed out of our house for the first time in a couple of days due to the massive amount of snow we were 'given'. Stir crazy was slightly the name tag we should have been all wearing, that and mine should have said HEAD COLD. We dropped Abe off to a birthday party, something I never did when Jason was here on a Saturday, as he worked that day. I no longer have that excuse, and let's face it, these kids need a freaking good time whenever possible!

Maybe it was being stir crazed, maybe the head cold coming on, maybe it was that we were in a minivan for way too long of periods yesterday...at any rate, we are driving along and I heard Oscar say possibly the most prolific thing, seemingly reading my mind for the last 10 minutes, 10 days, 3 months. I hear him say to Abe, "...would you just stop talking?" I had to resist the urge to LAUGH OUT LOUD! Those five words have entered my head on nearly a daily basis in the last 3 months...the act of saying it, I always imagined would be as liberating as doing a cartwheel, not wearing a bra, or drinking all day long...(I have very low standards).

Being that honest, in the moment...knowing that you are mentally nearing the wall and politely giving a heads up to the person next to you that you will BLOW IT if pushed much further (Chase Mortgage Co. that would be directed at you). Knowing that as much as life sucks at times, that's life- and you either learn from it and move on, or you stay stagnant and miserable. The last 3+ months have taught me a lot, however, they have seemed so much longer than that. Being burnt out and not having someone to fall back on is something I have to not only expect in my situation, but also have an arsenal ready to combat it. I'm getting better at seeing the 'enemy', now I just need to fight, and be ready to never claim defeat in 'Mental Jenga' or whatever the hell else life slings at me...all the while knowing that five words or less could get me through-and hand gestures while effective, are not necessary...

### ...wallowing, and hair bands...

...so, it's wallowing day...it's not found on your Hallmark list of holidays, but never-the-less it has attached itself to my ass and it's not leaving without a fight...everything is a reminder, and he is everywhere, but where he should be...

You know, in hindsight (which is always perfect, and in my current situation pisses me off to no end) I never appreciated all that I had with him. I never appreciated how someone who knew you better than yourself could make you feel, just by a look. I never told him how I loved that he knew all my stories. I never appreciated how he knew how to help me, and even more when it drove him nuts when he couldn't. I never appreciated all that he did for me, and frankly, I was lucky to have him and probably didn't deserve him...Now, he would be the first one to tell you that I put up with a lot of stuff from him too, and there you go, most men would never even admit that...why is that old adage so true, yet you can never do anything about it until it is too late, "...you don't know what you've got, until it's gone..."

Sadly, when I utter those words, that completely crappy 80's hair band Cinderella says it in my head...as if the saying wasn't horrid enough. But crappy 80's band or not, the saying is what I am currently living, and trying like the dickens to run away from every minute of my life...I have a complex inner narrative, usually it involves pretending that everything is fine will make it be fine...and up until now, it has distracted me sufficiently...

Until this afternoon...sort of like a drop in barometric pressure. I knew it was coming, thought I had battened down the hatches, but to no avail, it hit...the kind of sad that is deep from within. Where the tears start about your ankles and then have to reach your eyes slowly and tediously draining you, but all the while you know you have to let it out or else you'll drown...it all hits you, yet again. By this point you know how to swim, hell you've taught the course and you are certified by the Red Cross, but it doesn't matter...you've forgotten your training, and you're flailing at the edge of the water...suddenly, you remember...just float.

I'm not sure what brought this day on...every day is a reminder that you need to live life to the fullest, but it also is a harsh reminder to appreciate everything you have, when you have it...because when it is gone, there is nothing but an ache, nothing but a memory, nothing but a feeling that you once had...and while knowing you had it should be enough, it never fully quenches your thirst for more...and all you're left with are wallowing and crappy 80's hair-bands...

**...free cookies and Daddies at the Hy-Vee...**

...so, when you see Daddy, tell him to come up and see me...when are we getting a new Daddy...So, if Daddy is never coming back from heaven, who is going to be our Daddy? I thought I was doing a pretty good job. But, I'm 5'3", not able to lift things over my head easily, and clearly missing the 'Daddy' parts to make me relevant...so, now what?

Clearly, I have been waiting for this day...the day of questions. The day of questions that I could not possibly answer...if was just sort of figuring that they would be spread out, which they have. BUT, today, was ALL questions...as if life with a three year old isn't challenging enough...oddly, today I wasn't only fielding her questions, but also my 7 year old...with him it was rather statements that caught me off guard...

It started in the pre-pre-dawn hours, when Abe had a dream that he was in a closet with someone who was planning to eat him? Okay. The thing with this kid is, when you get up, even to go to the bathroom, his internal clock says, GOOD MORNING- no matter the time...so, what started as an early morning, quickly turning into an early start to questioning...what was life all about? Were we going to live in this house forever?

What's for breakfast? When are we getting a new Dad, I'm ready? It's the last one that threw me for a loop. I've heard such ramblings from my three year old, mostly because she is inquisitive, mostly because she likes the sound of her own voice- all the while, I was figuring that she didn't really know what she was asking...but from Abe, it was a head scratcher...

While I am proud of the mother I have become (at times not so proud of the routes I take), there is a certain magic about having a MALE in this house...it's like the mood changes, the atmosphere is filled with something else, possibly for my kids, something familiar that hasn't been around. They become rowdy and loud (more than normal), chatty and 'show-off-ish'. While I have known for months that something is missing at 815 Washington, tried my damnedest to create a 'normal'...the mere presence of a male has not gone unnoticed.

The funnier thing is hearing a three year old solution to our current vacancy..."...Mom, all you have to do, is go to Hy-Vee and just buy a Daddy there, and before we leave I can get a cookie..."-priorities, you know. After this suggestion, it leaves me wondering which is more comedy, explaining to her why I can't 'buy a Daddy' at Hy-Vee or the concept of finding a Daddy...both leave me more than a little speechless- no small challenge I thought. Then come the questions of when we are having another baby "for Atti to play with?" I informed them (Nora and Abe-who is baby crazy anyway) that without a Daddy, there will be no babies- all the while holding my breath that I wasn't opening THE CAN of worms that I'm not particularly ready to discuss with a 7 and 3 year old. I told Nora, "...well, what are your plans? You can't play with Atti?" To which she informed me she had better things to do...

As if the daily worries of this house don't weigh enough on my brain...now half my kids are looking to get me on "The Dating Game" just so they have someone to wrestle with around the house? ...great, just add it to the list of things to do during my free time...whenever I find out where the hell that is...

**...Friday nights and low lights...**

...so when you are a mom, it's like you are permanently in this certain world...you venture out occasionally, but not enough to remember what it was like before you earned stretch marks and lost your first name...and it is rare to have those opportunities. I mean, you can pick up your kids from school in a halter top with a cocktail in your hand, but it doesn't really bode well for your reputation...

Even when mothers go out together, sooner or later the discussion turns to coupons or grocery stores, indoor play grounds or Chuckie Cheese...and there is no disrespect in saying this, it's our day to day, and word of mouth is sometimes the best way to find things out. Currently, in my situation, I feel as though at times I am being swallowed up by "motherhood"...when the only time I get to read 'adult' material is at the dentist office, I need to shake things up a bit...put on clothes that I **DO** care if a child blows their nose on, pull out the heels, slap on some make-up, and get out the cookie flavored lip-gloss!

So, Friday, I got dolled up, had some SAINTED LADIES come over and watch my kids for the night (my kids couldn't wait for me to leave, and I'm fairly certain I didn't even say good- bye to them), and met up with some ladies...the best part was, all of these ladies I knew would be FUN. Just the kind of fun I required- some knew each other, some didn't, and by the end of the night we were all hugging- 'cause that's what girls do when they are a little over served, it's in our DNA...

The best part of the night, there was no discussion of play groups, no coupons, NO KID TALK really...as we sat and laughed, and ate, and drank adult drinks...it was possibly the best time I have had in a WHILE. A recharge of who we once were before we had to sensor ourselves for little ears...a time to tell stories, ask questions, and not really care how loud we were. We bonded in this low lit lounge, over how we knew each other, what we'd been through, and gave little thought to how we would recover the next day...you know the best sort of time!

Thankfully, after my recharge night I am finally feeling back to normal, flushed with a feeling of knowing that it was necessary to get a little silly, grateful for the chance to be a 'non-mom' for an evening and looking forward to planning another get together, just giving our livers a little time to heal, and ready to tell more stories...and for those who were there- I am so very lucky to have you!

## ...ice pops and silver linings...

...it's that time again, the time I sit down and write and have a billion things running through my head...ironically, nothing to do with the loss we have gone through, rather the challenges that I feel are on the distant horizon. The winds of change that come without the ability to control them, and the lack of control on your destiny. I've related a lot of what I'm going through to swimming, now as if swimming without floaties wasn't hard enough, I have to somehow let go, and know that life will fall into place...yeah, my OCD has no problem with that...

I started this whole thing with NO KNOWLEDGE, and really not claiming that I have any more than I had before...Jason did the business side of our life, I did the house stuff, small bills, and groceries. Ignorance is a word that sounds about right, but doesn't even come close. I've had to start from scratch, learn what the hell to do, and try to put it into practice. However, there are those questions/conversations/decisions that you don't take lightly, let alone discuss with yourself...and then it starts all over again...

It's such a minuscule thing, a conversation...but, when you think back on your life, how many conversations changed what you did, how you felt about something? How many conversations did you start feeling bewildered, and ended feeling bold, brave or even satisfied that you were doing the right thing? Having someone to bat around ideas, fears, and problems with is something that should be not only celebrated, but cherished...not many people understand the power that is behind that, I however, understand it all too well...

Sure, I never want for talking to someone in this house, yet the one who speaks the most is three years old, and I'm just not confident in her financial advice, let alone the last time she washed her hands...not someone you want to throw any heavy ideas on. The funny thing is, if I could just adopt a mindset like her, I'd be less stressed out, find the humor in most everything, and eat nothing but ice pops all day long...I need a second opinion.

When the need for 'letting go' is screaming into your face, how is it possible to not feel threatened because you just want a little control on your life? I find myself looking up and asking Jason, "Okay, now what? Where next? What should be the next plan of attack?"...at this point paying bills, making meals, doing laundry, changing diapers-that's sums up my control. Meanwhile, I know I'm being told to calm the hell down, take it day by day and it'll all come together...

While I have to start this mantra somewhere, knowing WHERE we'll end up or even a notion of that, for now, is what is making life more difficult than what we may be missing. But there is an up note-THE SILVER LINING. I have to remind myself (besides calm the hell down) is when I need the help...I know I will have friends there for me, because thus far, they have been the best things that have fallen into my place...

**...runner's high and gin-n-tonics...**

...the word that best describes how I was
feeling four months ago today is bleak...I
remember coming out into a room full of
some of his friends, having to tell them that
it was time...it was time to say anything they
might want to say to him, as this was the
end. I told them that what they might see
would not be something they want to
remember, and if they wanted to say
something to him from where they sat, that
was okay too...

At that dark point in my life, little did I
know how valuable those people would be
to me, moreover, I wouldn't have even been
able to comprehend how all of these other
wonderful, thoughtful, life changing people
would suddenly appear in my
life...unknowingly filling a void with just the
simplest of gestures. The smallest of things,
at just the right time, can take your psyche
from devastated to habitable. While it is at
times easier to wallow, having people in
your life that can raise you up, is rare, rich,
and prized.

I've never been a runner, unless I was being
chased (buh-dum-dum-ching), however,
lately it seems I'm running a race with

myself...hoping that at some point 'runners-high' will just kick in already, and the rest will be effortless and apparent. But nothing worth learning, is ever uncomplicated. These prized people I have above mentioned, they are the masses of people standing on the side of the race route, handing me water and cheering me on to the next marker...what they are doing may seem simple enough, but to me it's so much more than that, especially on my 'dark day'...

Everyone is allowed a 'dark day' in their lives. The fact that you are breathing in and out allows you to have one. With these days, you do with what you can, always hopeful that one day it might mean something different or better still, it will go from monthly to yearly. That being said, my 'dark day' has changed over the last four months, mostly due to the lack of time, space, kid-free zones, and basically life as I know it. And, it has changed partly (and thankfully) to these extra special people in my life, which four months ago, I would have never believed I would be so blessed to have. The check-ins, the hilarious texts, or the messages just letting me know that I have someone there if I need them...only one word can describe this: monumental.

So, on this fourth 'dark day' I have had in the last calendar year, I feel it deserved to fix a gin and tonic (as Jason would), and not only think of the person I was blessed to have in my life, but to celebrate all the new people that are making my life better with the simplest of gestures...

### ...brooding and 'slim jims'...

...so, today was one of those rare, unusual days where I had time alone with Abraham Archer (a.k.a Abe). We are starting the exhilarating and costly world of orthodontia. After they basically scared the crap out of him and me with the ins and outs of what we were venturing into, let alone having me sign a waiver saying I would keep up my end of the deal. They also had a LONG talk with Abe, telling him his responsibilities...really? This kid would never shower unless forced, let's put straight CASH into his mouth and make him promise to live up to his end of the bargain, with a simple, "Yes, I will..."? The whole thing got me thinking...

I have never spoken to my kids like they were kids...I never really realized this, until my friend April brought it to my attention a long time ago. So, that being said, they don't really speak like 'kids', rather creepy (at times) miniature adults. Now I am grateful for this, as I can use all the conversation I can get, it sort of bites you in the buns at times. So, these kids are not only able to carry a conversation, indubitably, these kids can argue their heads off, usually over nothing, at any given moment, all because I gave them this fantastic gift of language...I'm contemplating only signing to Atticus, just to cut down on the volume and the need for a cocktail...

Second of all, seven seems to be the new twelve. The level of disdain and seemingly acute embarrassment...mixed with the under-cutting feeling that, while yes, you are my parent, you know nothing...so, please don't speak, don't ask me questions, basically pretend we aren't together. Such a warm feeling to get from someone you were in labor for 20 hours to bring into this world. So, I figured he not only needed the time alone with me, he needed to be heard 'mano e mano'...he maybe would turn around. Nope. So, I accepted it, a little rattled, but I accepted it and figured I'd keep trying...

So, after our wonderful orthodontic adventure, shaken and not yet stirred, we went on to the other errands at hand, hoping I could glean some sort of 'positive' out of the day. I gave him the chance to choose at the grocery store some of the things we would buy...little did I know he only wanted doughnuts, cinnamon rolls, fruit roll ups, and chocolate milk. So, I handed him our list, tried to appease some of his 'wish list' and attempted to teach him how to shop. Having him pick out the cheapest of what we needed, whilst hoping that we were going to be able to connect, even in the simplest of forms. We made it to the checkout, after having lengthy conversations about how it would be easier to live in Quincy than Canton, the need for 87 different cereals, the disadvantage to buying 12 bags of chips, and the ins and outs of why anyone had to drink milk. We threw our Lenten promise away, as we'd already had the be-Jesus scared out of us, and he was rewarded a 'Slim Jim' (yuck, by the way). I figured it was a figurative cocktail for me...then it dawned on me.

This kid was my SIDE KICK just a couple of years ago...I mean, this kid was my shadow, my helper, my conversation exchange...He helped me clean, change sheets, my errand boy when Nora was a baby. It dawned on me, not only had he grown up, he'd sort of been replaced by a substandard girl. Don't get me wrong, where Nora is the consummate conversationalist, she is seriously lacking in the 'helping out around the house' end of things, nothing like Abe. Abe could have skipped kindergarten and went straight into cleaning house for someone, and he was excellent at it and loved doing it.

Never-the-less, he had been replaced as the older kid at home, and it never dawned on me before...this kid really needs time out by himself. If for nothing else than to be rewarded for the great help he was while home...rewarded for the great kid (even though he's got that brooding thing going) that he is...rewarded that he might always be the 'middle kid', by far he's helpful, imaginative, and loving, with the most contagious (and costly) smile my world...

**...clichés and caged birds...**

...so, it isn't some new cracked notion, but
lately I miss taking care of an adult. Funnily,
enough, taking care of four kids could
STILL make me want to take care of an
adult...I'm not sure if it's the gratification
that you get by doing it, the validation that
you get by doing it, or just simply who I am,
me. Whatever the case, it has made me
deeply ponder my past, present and
future...but not without a little help.


So, on the day that marked four months
from Jason's passing, I kept having clichés
come into my consciousness. I would be
doing something, resembling nothing (my
day to day) and BOOM, one would pop into
my head. At first, it was annoying, and then
it became funny. Jason and I would rarely
fight, however, whenever we would have a
slight argument, he would start talking in
clichés? I don't know why, but instead of
telling me what was on his mind ('cause let's
face it, I clearly and possibly to my fault,
have no problem saying what's on my
mind), he would start unconsciously talking
in clichés. While it would annoy the piss out
of me, usually it would just crack me up,

because he didn't even know he was doing it, and then the argument would be done...

For whatever reason, the phrase, "I know why the caged bird sings" has also been coming into my head for the last couple of days. I thought I understood the meaning of it, but I Googled it, just to be safe...turns out, I don't feel caged as much as **been given clarity**. I feel like I know why the caged bird sings, being taken care of is reassuring, bolstering and slightly more care free than where I currently sit...Caring for someone else, gives you this feeling, empowerment, accomplishment, at least it does for me. Taking care of someone, I feel reminds you your alive...and while I'm lousy with people to take care of in this house...

Anyone who has ever dated knows the rush you get when you first start dating. You have endless things to talk about. You sort of prattle over them. You seemingly are beyond preoccupied with this person, and then you get comfortable with each other, and that heady feeling sort of goes by the way side...It's the time you remember, the middle you sort of forget, and the present is just where you reside. But why?

Currently, I reside in a place where I value what I don't have...knowing my weaknesses, valuing my strengths, and understanding that this is what makes up the person that I am. I feel like I am setting a mental precedence: the giddiness, the gush, and all that goes along with it, should ALWAYS go along with it. Not just get comfortable and let go of that...that's where the magic is...who wouldn't want that every day? Someday, I've decided, as these are things that I clearly deal with daily (noted-HEAVY SARCASM), I'm giving and I'm settling for nothing but...

**...landmines, freight trains, and being reminded you are surviving...**

...so, here we go again...it's wave time...or I'm running a race...or whatever other cliché best describes my day to day life...it's sort of boiled down to survival of the fittest at times, and when your best friend comes to visit, the day they go home can be sort of a bummer...

I have this tendency to get trapped in my head, I don't mean stuck, I mean wearing-the-flannel-shirt-like-the-Unabomber-without-the-beard...I play a good game, and I can put on a convincing face. But it's those few people that know, while they can appreciate your 'craft' they are willing to be there when the bottom falls out, and know how to build you up. I am guilty of behaving this way, and I'm also very grateful I have a friend who not only knows me but can appreciate that this is just my way of DEALING.

April has seen the very best and worst of me. Jason, I don't think, could understand our relationship: our multiple hour chats on the phone, the long nights of laughing and telling stories (as if we hadn't told them all before). He did however, know how much it meant to have her (and her husband) in our lives...We've been nearly mugged, ridden a freight train in the quest of a good time, been nannies together, had to survive in less than survivable moments. In those moments, or the aftermath, you realize there was a reason this person came into your life so long ago. While you didn't understand it at the time, this person was MEANT for you, and I thank God for her every night.

My best description of when April comes to visit...it's like we (all in this house hold, as she is treasured by my kids as much as she is by me) are on a cruise! We have the best time, laugh, we eat the best food, play games, tell stories, laugh, I have a grown-up to drink/talk/cry/ LAUGH with, and at times we don't even have to get out of our pajamas! My kids have someone **new** to tell stories to, show Legos, discuss how 'Hogwarts' would really be, color pictures with...basically, a breath of fresh air where at times, let's face it, can get rather stagnant. Being able to talk to someone, when you need to, the fact that they understand not only all about your past, but really who you are, and not scared to tell you where they think you should go, as only a great friend can...

Coming here is also an education for her too...Atticus, will someday work for some Government Secret OPS department, as he leaves toys strewn like landmines, ready to trip you at any moment. Nora and her incessant talking, telling stories, and having to announce your name before she can ask you your 154th question of the morning. Abe, always wanting to act like he's doing a set at a comedy club, the only thing missing is the brick wall behind him. Oscar, wanting to go quid-pro-quo on any topic, NEVER, and I do mean NEVER, stumping April the entire time she was here-priceless for the mom who supposedly knows nothing...

The fact that she's seen me at my worst, seen me act pretty stupid, still calls me a friend and we can laugh every time we are together like we are teenagers again-that's more than a gift...it is a vacation from my insanity, a trip to the beach for my psyche, and gives my heart/head a break from wondering if I am doing alright...thank you is all I have to say.

## ...treachery, I know thy name...

...so, it's nearly here...spring. After my long sorted love affair with winter, we have ended our relationship if for nothing more than all the damned snow days we endured this year...the heart wants what it wants! The birds seem to know it's near, and I've made lots of promises around here about "when it gets warmer out, we'll...." Unknowingly, to those promised, it's more ammunition for them to freaking shower! But, with this new season, we'll hopefully see all that can be new...we've never seen this house in full bloom outside...We can get the porch swing up, and hopefully blow the old stink off of us...starting a new chapter in our lives, seeing as Winter was long and treacherous...

I've noticed that there are a few things I need to learn, and a few things I need to learn to appreciate...I may never get to actually eat a meal, fully, again. I'm not begrudging it, as it might be why I've lost weight. When SPEED FEEDING and 13 month old (when he's finished, it's WWF up in here), getting up to get the million things you never 'think' you'll need at mealtime, or even having to share my meal because it, "...looks better" than what one of my kids might be eating. By the way, we are eating the same thing...The ability to fall asleep at any given time, in any position, anywhere. I'm the sole reason they put the warning labels, "...may cause drowsiness, do not operate heavy machinery..." Yeah, that's me. The linguistic prowess of what a 13 month old wants at any given moment. Taking a 5 minute shower, even though you know an extra 7 minutes would be wonderful, but dealing.

Having a four cup coffee mug, and knowing the moment you fill it, you might actually drink all of it. These are the things I have learned to appreciate, humble but compelling. It's the things that I DON'T know how to do that have me stumped... So, I'm just going to throw some words out at you...**Plumbing. Lawn care. Fuse panels. Electricity. Rodents. Body hair. Penises. Puberty**...now I'm not saying I need to BE a man to know how to handle any of the above mentioned words, however being a man, it might be easier to explain some of these words, and let's face it would just come in handy. And cut to me, looking for 'how-to-books' on pretty much all of the above, not realizing that I had a secret weapon in my hand the whole time MY PHONE...the next time any of the above ensues I can either call it in, or GOOGLE it...

With the air of Spring upon us, certain things are being noticed...Abe has decided that he does INDEED need to learn to read, as well, it's a helpful thing to know how to do...he goes around my house like some eighty year old man who is judging his eyesight, reading any label he can. Oscar, while always fashion forward (will no longer wear skinny jeans, but has decided that it is okay if I do, um thanks) is completely hung up on his appearance...what's cool? What's not? Staring at himself in the mirror intently...still have to remind him, if they can smell you coming, the rest doesn't matter. Nora carries this stuffed animal around with her where ever she goes, the one who wanted to go outside and pee? Yeah, well, now he's not big on my cooking, I told her I was glad to hear it...

Lastly, the one who is changing the most, and I'm looking most forward to sharing spring with is Atti! Let's be honest, this kid will probably end up in the back of a squad car someday, but at least all of his tattoos will be spelled correctly. He is everywhere fast. He is the fastest learner I've had. He loves to be a little show off. And just recently, he has started giving hugs...well, and humping you as he does it. While my gal April was here, I showed her that he hugs, and she sort of said, "...what's with the rest of that?" I informed her, it was the most action I'd had in months, I'll be ignoring the action for the greater good...and just know spring is here.

### ...owls, Adele, and divas...

...owls and random bits of songs...that's what I'm left with tonight. The thought of him is fluttering through my head, with an all-day migraine, two 'smalls' that woke too early and didn't nap, and a school program where his absence, I am hoping, was noted by only me...my cocktail tonight? I'm drinking it neat...

For the last month, I have heard an owl, every single night. At times it is faint, tonight, it seems it was perched atop my chimney, 'whooping' away for about 30 minutes. Finally, I was like, "I get it already!" It seems I require a sledge hammer to the head to see signs anymore, but tonight, I GET IT! At times when I hear this owl, my mind sort of wanders...yet, he always comes to mind when I hear it...it's got to stand for something? It's not like I live in the woods...this is Canton, MO!

Tonight was the last school program of the year, and wow, just getting out the door was a DOOZIE! The always fashion conscious Oscar, initially came down in some every day garb with a tie. I quickly informed him, I'd ironed something for him to wear. He tells me he'd like to see it, as if he had a million De La Rentas in the wings waiting for him to try on...I told him the choice was his, he'd wear what I ironed or he'd go in his underwear. FURY!! FURY, hath a diva scorned! He quickly earned 3 strikes, and was warned we were coming up on a weekend, he'd might want to not have to be 'Amish' for the whole thing.

Abe, he found the whole evening as his 'Open-Gym' night, scurrying around everywhere once we got to the school. I let it go, until I looked up, and was utterly embarrassed by both he and his brother acting like they just downed a case of JOLT Cola. I went up to Abe and told him to come back to his seat, and informed him that he would now be as embarrassed as I was by his shenanigans, and that I was going to make him hold my hand walking back to our seats...worked like a charm...at least for a little while.

This whole thing wouldn't be a big deal...it's just a school program, but clearly we are still missing parts of our family. We look as if we are intact, but look closer and there is still something missing...and it is magnified in my kid's eyes, I see it, it tears me apart, and there is nothing I can do about it. Seemingly also, there is always someone that you bump into who has to bring up the fact that we are working on a different format than we were when they first met me at the beginning of school. Yeah, I knew that already, thank you for reminding me. BUT, it's understandable, people don't know what to say.

When you are missing something in your life, everything else seems, again, magnified. There isn't anything small that you can do to fix it. It's the hole in the wall that you can see, you can't reach without a 30 foot ladder, and even if you could, you'd have no idea how to fill it. It's just staring at you, gaping, massive and ugly. So, you find new things to look at, you sit in a different spot in that room, or don't even go in it at all...it doesn't fix the problem, just makes it go away for a little while.

Then there are the random bits of lyric that have filled my head, at times in a way that is eerie, others when I feel like I just needed to be reminded of it...For the last two weeks, it has been an Adele song. Today, a dear friend stopped by to 'look me over' as she put it, and hands me a biography on....Adele. I was sort of speechless, and thought to myself, 'hey, dumb ass, pay attention!' There she was in all her glory, Adele, the woman who has been singing the same six words in my head for the last two weeks...here was another owl, just not flying through my house crapping and scaring the children, but being handed to me. I feel as though, I now have this cosmic obligation to myself and my children to not only pay attention, but to put what's right, right. Deal with what I can handle, because **clearly**, someone else is handling the rest. While it scares me, baffles me, and petrifies me all at the same time...I just need to sit back and remember, it's being handled...

## ...Promises, promises

...well, I think between the mixture of snow, flu, and lack of SPRING LIKE temperatures...I might have failed my Lenten promises...paying attention to all the little things I did, but when the days grow long because: your kids praise-the-sun-up, do not nap, are little destroyers, sass talkers, arguers...you sort of start counting down until bed time mentally. At times, my countdown starts earlier in the day than it should...But faced with that 'guilty-mother-thought' I did however glean some things out of my last 40 days. I gleaned it as I was trying to shut my exhausted eyes for 20 minutes, worked out well, huh?

Turns out, in those weary 20 minutes I came upon what I actually already knew, but in a way that sort of made sense. I should know my kids, right? I'm their mom, they came out of me, this shouldn't be some time altering revelation...However, I have been guilty of completely OVER DISSECTING my children in the last 4+ months. As a mother, there are some things you just can't control, shield, or help your kids through unless they are ready...some are, some pretend they are, and some are not.

Oscar has this creative imagination that leaves him clueless...he's clueless to some common courtesies, he's clueless about his size (which I am grateful for), he's clueless about math, mainly because it's about the FACTS, not what you could create with them, just the facts. Knowing this, I should know that he will be the slowest kid on earth to get his shoes on, he will take longer to do most everyday processes, mainly because he's thinking how he would do them if he were Harry Potter...and I love him for that.

Abraham has quite an imagination, but is completely obsessed with the facts, he loves math, hates reading, and is all about finding solutions and figuring out problems. Probably the reason I ask him to do simple tasks around the house, because I know I won't have to explain it, diagram it, or remind him of what he's about to do...he's my helper, and I love him.

Nora's imaginary world is so vivid, let's face it it's better than her day to day life. At times this is interesting as she talks nonstop, and enjoys starting her day with some phrase...example, as I was handing her Gatorade today, hoping she'd keep it down, she says to me, "I haven't had this in AGES!"...clearly, she skips the fence on her real world/imaginary world as she's never had Gatorade, but clearly knew what she was saying. Her days are filled with swimming lessons, music school and ballet classes, all of which happen in her head, and she's happy to do it there...I tell her every night that she is my best friend.

Atticus likes to create problems to see the outcome, all the while knowing that he shouldn't be in that cabinet. Putting an entire package of maxi pads in the toilet and running away laughing, me not knowing what he is laughing at and finding them HOURS later. Climbing out of the highchair-balancing on one leg and looking at me-smiling. Figuring out how to move around the furniture so that he can get the remote for the TV and running away as fast as he can...and this is all before 11 am. Atticus is all about the reaction. Sometimes it's worth one and sometimes he doesn't WANT to know it...but his dimples and laugh keep me young and remind me that I will be rewarded when he has his own children someday...

Knowing all of this, I still mentally count down the day until the house is quiet. When I'm left with MY thoughts, feeling selfish, but hoping that this is just my way of coping the fact of being out numbered. The times I really feel like I hit the wall (the last 24 hours for example), I have a little chat with myself and Jason, say a couple of expletives, make a couple of bargains, and keep moving. Hopefully through coping (and talking to myself, healthy, huh?), I can somehow remind myself that there will be good days, bad days, days without dessert, and days when promises will be missed and ones where they are kept...I might not know where I'm going, but I know who I am going with...

**...rock, paper, scissors...**

There are things in this life you have to deal
with...bills, laundry, groceries, meals,
cleaning...these are things that have to be
done for you to thrive, survive, or just live.
There are some things that never come into
your active consciousness, however, that
you know are there, whittling away...that
must be dealt with, but even when it's like a
road sign that you pass on the highway, you
are still left wondering. Like trying
something for the first time with no picture
or directions to help you understand, you
wing it still wondering...like trying to
explain something you not only do not fully
comprehend, you babble what sounds best,
still wondering...Did I do it right?

You grow up, knowing what you know,
learning along the way, hopefully figuring
out who you are, and where you fit in. You
can explain what you are knowledgeable
about, but hopefully have the presence of
mind to know when to say, "I don't know",
as that will only help you learn, grow, and
become a better-rounded human being. You
find people, as you make your way through
life, which not only you can learn from, but
compliment you in such a way that you are
profoundly a better person for knowing

them. You, at some point, will have to understand where your strength comes from, where you can loan it, and how you can pay it forward in such a way that is genuine and sincere. You understand also, at some points in your life, you will have to borrow that strength, and there is no shame associated with that. You are made up of the best parts of those who brought you into this world, and even those who came before them. You are a treasure, and you will need to remind yourself of that....kids, this is the long and short of life, what you do with it is up to you.

Funny thing around here, the Talls now standard way to settle any serious, intelligent dispute: rock, paper, scissors. It's seemingly the 'go-to' way to settle most any conflict. Four o'clock woes? You rock, paper, scissors it. Who gets the remote? You rock, paper, scissors it. Last chocolate Pop Tart? ...and so on. When I hear this supreme form of justice being used, I have to appreciate an 8 and 7 year old's brain...and simultaneously envy it. No matter how many times you tell them to just enjoy being a kid (Jason would say this to them at least 3x a week as well), none of it makes sense until you are not. My woes fall into the category of how much they have had to grow up since November, with no choice, sadness, and some anger...they are these amazing, small people who have had to deal with something so adult...no rock, paper scissors could possibly solve, and as their parent it sort of tears at me.

Things like these enter my head, but I'm already an adult, I tend to babble, and at times my kids look at me like they'd rather not know me. I'm fairly preoccupied with hoping that I am doing it right. Slightly flawed by not knowing if there are second chances…Merely consumed by the notion that I am going to screw my kids up…Bemused at how life will be in a year…Praying that at the end of the day, what my kids snicker and laugh at when I say it to them jokingly (albeit, said in a voice of a whiny mom), "...make good choices..." My hope, is somehow these three words could be the precursor or could somehow resonate years from now, when rock, paper, scissors just won't do...

**...by the way, I love you...**

...so, it was five months ago...a call in the wee hours of the morning, rushing to get dressed, heading to the hospital, all the while knowing my worst fears had come true...a feeling like you were getting ready to go head on into something that you had no idea how to handle it or even wanted to. I remember talking to a few scant people on the phone once at the hospital, and they kept saying, he's going to rally, he's going to come through...but I knew he wasn't, and I knew not only my heart, but I myself would never be the same. The rest is sort of a blur, not because I don't remember what happened, I vividly remember those next twelve hours as if they just occurred...but I feel like my psyche has made them a blur if for no other reason than to cope.

However, during that time I remembered having a dream two days before, during the slight nap I took. I was sort of standing back, watching the hustle and bustle of the hospital's main lobby...all of the sudden, I see Jason. He walked out from my right side, never looking in my direction and headed straight out the sky bridge, out of the hospital. During the dream I remember thinking, he's going to come out of this.

Then it dawned on me, on that last day, he's already come out of this, days before, and has gone to the other side. It's a chilling thought, some might think crazy, but now I feel like it was his way of showing me he was going to be alright...he was big on symbolism, and now that I think about it, it's sort of profound.

We have now been in this big house in Canton, MO longer without him than with him. At times in the last couple of months I have walked around here and thought, okay, now what? This house is perfect for us, but is that meant to be temporary? I think of all the things that flooded my head when we moved in, all the memories that I was looking forward to making with Jason here...and with that it is rather bitter sweet.

There is some sort of presence in this house, whether it be because of its age, the character, or just that our 'stuff' fit in it so perfectly...at times however, it made me feel like running away. Maybe by running away it would all make sense? As if getting out would fix something? So we did. We went away for Easter, visited my family, and despite a couple of us getting sick, we had the best time! I am lucky my family loves me as much as they do. There were quite a few pitches of how wonderful Indianapolis is. I especially loved the Indianapolis Monthly that laid on my bedside table, hint taken. The kids with their cousins and Indiana Grandparents, me with my sisters and brother, it was the kind of time that coined catch phrases, evoked giggles, and made memories...the stuff they make Hallmark commercials about. But, on the way home, I wondered, how would it feel walking back into our house? I mean after everyone using the bathroom, getting all of our crap unpacked, finding Nora some underwear, Atticus a pacifier, and locating where I put that one bag...it was instantaneous, this is our home...and for now, that is all that matters.

Once sorted out, we headed outdoors as it was beautiful out. The 'Talls' wanted to freak out the neighborhood kids by acting like they'd been playing all day while those sad sacks sat in school. This one boy who lives across the street was walking home. I waved to him, and he waved back to us and said, "Hi, Nora! Hi!"...she immediately was sort of turned to stone, as if she forgot thru the winter that this adorable 4th grader lived across the street. She had forgotten that she'd played football on his team in the empty lot. She'd forgotten that all fall she called him by the wrong name, and still can't say his name right...She greeted him, "...oh, Hi!" and then turned toward the sidewalk and said to herself, "...by the way, I love you..." I nearly fell down laughing, thinking of how crazed Jason would be if he saw that, freaking out that she was boy crazy and what will happen when she's 16?!?!...I figure, she can't get into too much trouble if she keeps talking to herself...

**...are we getting hormonal? It's a ball game...**

...so, the last few days have been interesting...I'd almost say manic at times. I'm not sure if it's the change in the weather. Watching the scenery from out our windows change daily as the earth starts it's slow warm up. The notion, that this was Jason's favorite time of year, he'd get seed catalogs months ago, but would be verbally planning some gigantic garden extravaganza in his head...only to grow a few things. The days are staying lighter a little longer...just changes all around.

Maybe it's 'about that time'...maybe it's like some twisted form of jet lag, you are seemingly doing okay, then the world pressurizes, and you aren't prepared. Ironically, the things that have hit me in the last few days, aren't the things I have always loved and just noticed again. They were the things that I learned to love through Jason's eyes...and they are coming around faster than a one-two-punch...crazy music, talking 'gardening', laughing with the kids about the silliest things...And it isn't just me noticing. Nora was pretty vocal today about how she was feeling, for me it just felt good not to be feeling it alone.

Today was also the opening day at Busch Stadium for the St. Louis Cardinals. I knew little about baseball before I met Jason...hell, I knew little about most sports before I met Jason. While he loved football and I don't, baseball was our middle ground. He took me to Cardinal games, taught me, well what he could teach a girl who is sports ignorant...and I loved it. So, today, I turned on the radio, like he would have, and listened to the opening ceremonies. All the pomp and circumstance any true baseball fan would love to see/hear if they got the chance to be there, on opening day. The famed Anheuser Busch Clydesdale's took the field, Fred Bird warmed up the fans, then they honored Stan Musial...and I stood in my kitchen...and lost it. I don't mean a tear, I mean full on ugly cry! Then just as suddenly, I started laughing. Had Jason been here, he would have said something along the lines of, "...are we getting hormonal? It's a ball game!"

So, tomorrow, we'll look out our same windows and we'll see what else has bloomed. We'll listen to more ballgames, have a beer with neighbors on the driveway, talk about gardening and with any luck learn to use the tiller so it isn't JUST talk. While the sum of these things, don't really add up to much, for me they are treasures of what once was, what can be and maybe a nudge (or a one-two-punch)from someone who you love that you just can't see.

### ...cage fighting, it happens...

It never fails...we order Chinese food, and the fortune cookies are always the best part of the meal for my kids...Maybe it's the way we've learned to read off the 'lucky numbers' in a Lotto announcer's voice. Maybe it's waiting on baited breath, hoping that our fortune is more compelling than, "You will have a party..." Maybe it's the hope for something more...However, it always includes Nora, handing her fortune to me, asking me to read it, as she takes the halves of the cookie, holds it to her ear and says, "...Mom? I can hear the ocean in here..." Clearly, she gets a special sort of MSG in her lo mein...but, she might just be onto something...

It seems like a lifetime. It feels like the last five months have been more like a year...and sadly, I have found out that all the cliché statements that you are told while grieving are...true. You have to 'take it day by day' and 'walk through' it and 'let yourself grieve'...however, whenever you are told these things by people (who love you but don't really know what to say to you) no one ever gives a time line. No one ever names a date, specifically, when it will all make sense. You find yourself at times happy, and wonder, "Okay, is it now?"...wondering if there will be a fall out later.

I think my way of coping was somehow subliminally instilled in me long ago, like when I was a child. I grew up in a funeral home, with a father, who somehow rarely ever got upset. He knew when to be reverent, he knew when to be compassionate, but his day to day didn't seem to affect him as far as any of us ever saw. I feel like somehow that was a lesson, very early in my life, in knowing that some things you just cannot change. Being bitter about your station in life doesn't always help your situation, things just happen. And while you would never want them to happen to you, you don't always get to make that choice. I am grateful for this childhood experience, some find weird, because in a very massive way it has helped me understand that my take on what I'm going through is very different than what others might think...It just happens.

In these five months I tried as much as possible to find the silver linings in things. While I've been stunted at what life will hold, and what will happen next, what do I do? Come to find out, I'm not in any control of that. Really. I remember my sister getting my mom a plaque that says, "Kathy, I've got this under control...~God". It's perfect, because it's true. It's not about the course you take in life, it's about understanding the whole thing is an adventure, and worrying about the details, you are surely bound to miss something wonderful. Those things you worry about, those things you have to go through? At the end of all this will make up who you are, with the biggest payoff...

In these last five months I have had to learn a lot about myself and my kids. I'm not going to lie, of course my life would be better if I weren't doing this alone. Of course my kids wouldn't have some convoluted notion that I am their mother as well as their DRILL SERGENT. And let me tell you, playing 'good-cop/bad-cop' alone, isn't any trip to the beach either...at times it's maddening. But, it happens, and you can either cave on them, or make yourself the **Self-Proclaimed-Mid-Mississippi-River-Cage-Fighting-Commissioner** and REGULATE! All the while knowing, while you might not be doing this the right way, or the way others would do it, you are doing it, and that's just the way it has to happen...

**...when Santa talks, dammit, you listen...**

...so, it's spring. Okay, well, that obviously has been established by someone other than me...anyway, this Spring has been wild, snow one day, 70 degrees the next...Six inches of rain, continuous, in eight hours...already damp ground, moist basement. It was inevitable, I literally dreamt last night that I could hear water pouring in below me...well, it wasn't a dream.

So, this morning, coffee in hand, baby fed and in bed, I dared...I 'power-sipped' my coffee, set it down, and walked toward my basement door. First of all, you should know, don't care for basements, or attics for that matter. I know they are there, that is the extent of our relationship...if I ever plan to be a realtor, I need to seriously BUCK UP! So, there I am, at the basement door, prepared? I opened the door, flipped on the light, and looked down the steps, there at the bottom, I see the snowflake shower mat, floating...awesome.

As I gained the courage to venture a little further down, the reality of what I was about to see set in...there was my Christmas tree, floating...plastic tubs filled with Christmas decorations, on their sides (sipping in water as if from a straw) floating... and I hadn't even stepped foot off the steps...I no longer needed coffee to wake up, I'd just been hit in the head with an invisible hammer.

I tried to stay calm. I tried to be blasé about it. I went on with my morning ritual of getting the kids ready for the day, but slowly, ever so slowly, it started sinking in. I got back down stairs with the kids, and told them about the water. I told them that we'd be calling the plumber and hopefully he could fix it, and as for the stuff down stairs, it was just stuff...it could be replaced. Abe immediately became emotional..."What about my 'Cage Fighter'??!!!" What? I calmly informed him, of all of the stuff we had in the basement, a plastic inflatable cage fighter would probably be the <u>only</u> thing that we'd be able to keep! Then it hit...then it started to sink in. The things I would probably have to throw out, the things floating in water for an undetermined amount of time would most likely be ruined, are some things that I cannot replace...not because I couldn't find them at Hobby Lobby, but because they were filled with memories...stuff is stuff, but memories...that gets tricky.

So, the plumber and his wife came. They are GODS, even though they started out in the basement yelling up at me that there was at least eight inches of water down there. It had risen since I power-sipped my coffee, cool. They not only told me they could fix the problem, but told me I needed to turn off my furnace, as the water was about an inch away from blowing it! "Turn it off for a while, we'll let 'er dry a bit, get this water down, and go from there..."

I offered them coffee, a cocktail, told them where the liquor was, if they WERE ever interested. I know I'd been since about 7:15 am...but, by this time, I resolved that whatever I would find down there was stuff...and at least we had a furnace!

Thankfully, my mother-in-law came over, so I could head down and start the clean-up, or out as the case may have been. The plumbers wife, sort of started picking tubs up and moving them to higher ground, which thankfully, we didn't really have that much down there. I opened the first tub, and it had been a floater, water logged, and wasted. I went through and got out what I could, and thought I'd come back to it. Then it was the same story with the other tubs...trying to pick out what wasn't ruined, laying them out to dry. I actually had to take apart glass ornaments and empty water out of them.

What was left were some ornaments, anything that I'd been smart enough to put in zip lock bags and stockings. Collections, gone. Special garland, gone...and that was fine. I was getting ready to move one tub outside. I picked up this water logged Santa, which somehow survived, and in his battery operated voice (of which I know I'd turned off when I put it away after Christmas), "...**Remember, the magic of Christmas, lies in your heart**..." Well, let me just tell you, I nearly CRAPPED MY PANTS!!! First out of fright! Next, out of the thought of how much Jason couldn't stand that thing. You had to hear it about 327 times a day, as some minion was always pushing it. However, finding it, and having it somehow say those words, to me, was perfection.

So, it's been quite a day, glad to see that it is over...proud of myself for getting it sorted out...grateful for mother-in-laws...VERY GRATEFUL for plumbers...Moreover, feeling lucky, that while the Spring rains of 2013 might have taken some of Christmas with them, the magic will be staying here...

**...with love ~ the Unabomber...**

...it's human nature I suppose...when things just seem to work, no meltdowns, no breakdowns, no terrorist plots before the sun comes up...things seem to be going in your favor, and then you suddenly halt yourself. It is in that moment when you realize either an anvil will, at some point, fall on your head OR one of the kids will come home with head lice...so you lie in wait.

The notion of using the phone has erupted in Oscar's brain, begging to call a friend daily for the past week. I give him the phone and realize, he has no idea what he's doing. I was answering a business line at his age. He finally gets his friend on the phone, and says, "...it's Oscar, yeah, okay. See you tomorrow"...that's it.

At times when you seem to be hurdling from one life-learning-lesson to another, you just reside in the notion that, this is in fact, your life. It's not glamorous, it's not pretty, it sometimes sucks, but the sun sets and then rises again, and there you are, stumbling to start the coffee at 5:30 am. The next 'want' is to get a little in you before the reason you are up this early wakes the dead. You see others, jovial, as if every day were some parade...and you think (only think, and just for a minute), "...aw, screw them..." The grass isn't always greener, and manure smells the same any time it's under your nose, right? But when you are in a place that isn't where you 'want' to be, things seem to be evaluated differently, move a little slower, and there always seems to be time for self-evaluation.

Meanwhile, in the life of a seven year old, Abe already has his second choice for prom lined up...he's in the first grade.
An old saying, that has been said to me at least once a week, was retold to me recently, in a slightly hilarious, slightly altered, yet very discerning way, "God wouldn't give me any more than he thought I could handle...I only wish he didn't think so much of me...".

While the ending always catches me laughing, the old adage is true. Life isn't perfect, for anyone. I know why/how people are capable of just losing it. There are times when I fear I am mentally just one flannel shirt away from living in a shack in the woods and signing Guy Fawkes Day cards "...with love~ the Unabomber". I get that people lose their shit...However, I know I will never make it to the cabin in the woods, I can't even use the bathroom without a little hand under the door, checking my whereabouts. Life is what you make of it...but when it's going, well, seemingly without injury, you question what the hell is going on?

In an alternate universe, where she is somehow the non-Spanish-speaking-all-knowing-queen-of-the-samba-dancers, there's Nora. I not only caught her singing, "...rumor has it...rumor has it..." today, she also told me she loved my nails, she hoped I won...sure.

I constantly have to keep reminding myself that this isn't sh*t that I have to go through, while it does suck and there is no control of it... It's sh*t I am ACCOMPLISHING and SURVIVING, all the while I've managed to remember to wear my underwear <u>under</u> my clothes. No one has head lice, no visible anvils, and thankfully Atticus hasn't figured out how to use doorknobs, yet...until then I lie in wait.

**...today I was Uranus...**

So, it is unofficially summer in this house. Today was the 'Talls' last day of school, and tomorrow we head out on our first summer adventure. The car is packed, the snacks stockpiled, and I have my mental game face on. However, there have been some moments in the last couple months that as a mom, are slightly indescribable...an ache in your heart, while trying to do your best, you know you dropped the ball...mainly because you have about 50 of them flying at you at once, and you realize something has got to give...

There are many times a week that I just wish there were more minutes in a day to make up for possible time lost. Those moments when you want to be one place for your kids, and realize that without some sort of time machine, it is impossible. As a mom, I hate missing out on things at school, but let's face it, my nanny is nonexistent, Nora WILL NOT shut up for more than 7 minutes unless drugged and while chasing Atticus is good exercise, it doesn't really allow you to enjoy a school program or award ceremony. The harder part of my life lately is having to weigh who's 'thing' is more important...I know we are not talking *Sophie's Choice* here, but when you are constantly trying to make your kids feel good about themselves not showing up for the little things adds up. Suddenly, you feel like the sub-standard crackers you try to pawn off to your toddler…They don't really know what tastes good, right? But when you get that look, the one you fear, the look of sub-standard-mom (SSM)...it stings a little.

I was planning this full-fledged EXTRAVAGANZA for when the 'Talls' got home. Soda, of course. They're favorite foods, vegetables optional, you know it. I believe I even yelled out the refrain of 'SCHOOLS OUT FOR SUMMER!!!' when they walked in the door. I have been running since 5:15 this morning, but damn it, when they walked in that door, it was going to be AWESOME. Now, part of this was for them, the part I could do anything about, the other part was for me, SSM. I offered them snacks, soda, told them what was for dinner...they asked to go to the neighbor's house. Okay. I asked them to first unpack their bags. It was then, Abe got all excited and announced, "...here it is, today I was Uranus!" and proceeds to show me a paper planet he wore in the off-off-off Broadway production they did today about the planets. However, maybe it was the lack of sleep, maybe it was having to shuffle the 'Smalls' around the Medical Group today, or maybe because it was just that funny...I busted out laughing. I quelled it quickly, only to look at Oscar, and he was laughing too. Abe said, "...yeah, I know what you are laughing at, but the costume was a cool green planet!"

It was then that I realized, this isn't the end. This isn't the day before my work evaluation, thank God. No one is finalizing the proper spelling on my epitaph, while my kids are getting ready to spit on it...there is still time to turn this around. While I know there will be more SSM days in my future, I might not be able to do anything about it, except make the best of it. A lot can be figured out in 3 months, and hopefully we can somehow, if nothing else, find a way to laugh about it...even if maybe we shouldn't.

**...real life?**

...well, I'm working on a 'skeleton crew'. The 'Talls' were given the chance to stay in Indiana for a couple of weeks and spend time with our family there. In the past, I would have been hesitant about them staying so long away from home. After the last 7 months, I feel like they not only need a little 'Tall' time, but the people they are with will be infinitely more fun than futzing around with me...truth is truth. So, even the thought of being down to two kids, sort of had me reeling a little...wondering, wait...what?

Two kids? How does that work? (...no, I'm not institutionalized?)

Ironically, it all still works...while the grocery bill will be a little lighter, it's not like having only two kids will afford me the chance to pee alone. Two kids make the same messes. Two kids still do not allow me to actually sit down longer than 2 minutes during a meal, not to mention the fact that one of them will only eat what I eat, and we are eating the same things. Now, having two kids who do not sneak out of their beds, two kids who don't find it necessary to be watching TV at 6:01 am, finally two kids who go to bed at 7 pm- BREATHTAKING!

I sit here in the relative church-like quiet of my house...thoughts racing, yet enjoying the near silence. I was reading Nora a princess story book tonight...and I found the whole thing fascinating. While these ladies had their trials and tribulations in finding their prince, always, always was there a happy ending...and seemingly quick.

No waiting around for years for the prince to show up, by that time their looks had gone and their one claim to fame was they made a mean meatloaf. Their princes came, they were as beautiful as the day they had originally met them, and insert happy ending. You never hear about what happened to them. You never hear how the prince got all fat, and liked to drink and be loud in public. Or how the princess yo-yo dieted to no avail, how her hair color resembled nothing found in nature, and more than once had she been seen at the grocery store with her skirt caught in her underwear...NOW, THAT IS REAL LIFE. It got me to thinking, what sort of messed up life are we portraying? Why is it that love/marriage is never portrayed as it should be? Work.

Now, if you are lucky, the work you have to do doesn't always resemble work. You can be a prince/princess that saves the day just by putting in the work. If you are really lucky, you are with someone who you not only honor, but also would even do extra 'work' and think nothing of it. If you are in this situation, seriously take a minute and appreciate it. Not everyone has it or appreciates it, and as I see it, any extra appreciation could never hurt you. If you do not have this, you should. You owe it to yourself to treat people/ be treated in this way, whether it's more work than you have in you...it's worth it. Ironically, I spend a lot of time thinking about this very topic. I find myself thinking about how I feel like I appreciated what I had, I probably could have done more at the time to show it. I find myself hoping that my own kids will somehow find this...Whether it be the chance for someone to love them like this, or the even greater ability to love someone in this way.

While loving someone doesn't always resemble some fairytale, you are ultimately the story teller, if the ending sucks, well...that's sort of on you. While I do live with a house of little people, my hair resembles that of a color found in nature... I'm not currently seeking a prince, just curious whether the rest of my story will be the blockbuster Disney re-make, or resemble more of something you'd see on a Monday Night Movie...

**...SAY BACKPACK!!!!**

...I'm not really a gambler. I'm a waste at a casino, I sit at a slot machine and play for the free drinks. Things that are perceived bad luck or unlucky have never really been an issue with me...I'm the opposite. Black cats, I'll stop for you. Broken mirrors, just affords me to not see my bad hair day. Lastly, the number 13? Well, I've got your number, because some pretty amazing things happened to me on 13ths...and now we are moving onto seven.

So it's been seven months, and I feel if I were working out of my home (because my kids had better never do this, I do their laundry) it would be just about time for a **'job evaluation'**. While, this is not entirely the same thing, I'm always to work on time, I never leave it...It has seemed fitting in the last couple of days to sort of reflect on what has gone on, what goals I haven't met and what has been accomplished. I feel like I would probably be marked poorly at times for a bad attitude/zero patience. Someone probably has over heard me using foul language, and again, they would remind me that drinking on the job, while it makes it tolerable, is sort of frowned upon...I, in response, promise to get a handle on it and remind them that in actuality, I was clocked out at the time...

Seven months of trying new things, trying old things, and trying to make things work. Some have been successes, some have been epic failures, and some will always be changing, as we change. Today, is the first time in seven months on the seventh that I have not been with all of my kids. Every month, while I try to make it special, I try not to make it totally obvious that the 'Shrine Circus' is in our living room, just a gentle progression of life moving on, never forgetting, but moving on.

With the 'Talls' out of town, life around here has been SERIOUSLY MODIFIED. All the shows that might annoy the 'Talls' the 'smalls' are eating up. Between Elmo shrieking about nothing, I've heard the phrase, "...SAY BACKPACK" so many times, I'm starting to mentally plot Dora the Explorer's demise. I realized we were getting near the end of the day, when I start hearing Nora talk to herself about how she has really got to drop the itch and needs some dandruff shampoo...meanwhile, Atticus is standing on the piano...what was the drinking policy again? At times in the last seven months I have felt the need to break out of here as if my pants were a blaze, not because I don't love every inch of my children or because I want to shirk my responsibility. A break is required. Then other times I sort of purposely isolate myself and my kids, almost seeming aloof, because

I feel like it is really in every one's best interest to stay away. Sadly, these are my issues. Having four kids under control is my NEMESIS! Chaos is something I am still working on embracing, and the sooner I do, my life will become infinitely easier. Not sure how that would be worded on my job evaluation? "...Put down the reformatory uniforms and have fun already..." or something along those lines.

At the end of this seventh, I'm thrilled that while my 'Talls' aren't here, they are having a blast at a baseball game...I'm thrilled that Nora finished her lunch, that she ordered herself and kept it down (strawberry milkshake and cheese fries-yikes)...I will never forget watching Atticus only wanting a milkshake for lunch (at one point he resembled a competitive eater), giggling the whole time, and never once getting brain freeze. For me, this seventh is just a reminder. A reminder that every month there is a little more laughter, my children are growing faster than I had ever imagined and possibly a little ownership (sort of in a backwards way), that I am actually pulling this off. Of course, I'm pulling it off with the help of family and friends, but I'm pulling it off...and it's a pretty heady feeling...as for the 'job evaluation', I must be pretty passionate about my job, I do it for free...


## ...sour mix needed...

...it's the thing I've been dreading...the thing I knew I would inevitably have to handle, being the only adult in this house...it's the one thing that I am embarrassed that I'm a COMPLETE chicken about...and the moment I smelled it, it was as if I could hear Jason laughing his ass off, knowing what a complete spaz I am...we had a dead mouse, somewhere...

Okay, well, at least I knew it was upstairs. I tried to talk myself out of it, but the smell got worse. I called the exterminator...they were too busy to get back to me. At this point, the smell was about too much for me. I took a deep breath, gathered the courage...and called my neighbor Jerry. I told him my woes, and reassured him that I basically needed him there for moral support. He came over, we located the smell and the rotting corpse and formed a plan of action. I'd like to say I picked it up and faced my fears- I'd like to say that. Jerry, amidst my slight yelling of "eeewww", took care of it. GOD BLESS HIM, and God bless a guy who will come over and do the dirty work for you. His payment? A whiskey sour for him and his wife...love thy neighbors.

I find it interesting, that I can get all emotional about something like a mouse, dead or alive. When other times I seem, and must seem to others, sort of like I'm missing a sentimental gene. I feel like at times I should be more sad, and nothing. Maybe it's a coping mechanism. Maybe it's because I've blocked myself from feeling that way. Maybe it's lunacy. What brought me to ponder this? I decided to look at some pictures the other day. It was the first time in a very long time that I've climbed up on a chair, got out a few photo albums, just sat down, and looked. It's strange how my reaction has changed by looking at old pictures. We all do it, we look at a picture of ourselves and silently critique it. My hair is a mess...what was I wearing? Why were we there again? Now, it's completely different. Now, it's like a focus on things I wouldn't have before, usually on the kids' reactions in the photo, or Jason's expression. The more photos I looked at, I realized that it's not painful like it was before. It's more seeing a picture, and suddenly you are watching an old 8mm home movie playing...all grainy, and slightly misty around the edges. You recognize the time at that moment...you can remember what it felt like...hear the laughter...smell the room around you, at that moment.

It's interesting how your memory can tap into something as simple as a picture, and you can be transported a little. It's not like I have to get the albums down to do that. I seem to look at a picture of Jason sometimes, and it's as if he's telling me something only I can hear, usually with his eyes. Generally, I laugh, as sometimes it's an inside joke I remember, a limerick you wouldn't want to say in open company, or just him encouraging me not to lose my s*#t yet, it's only 10:15 am!

I feel like sentiment is in the eye of the beholder...I have adopted a theory that I have tried to live closely by: there might be, at times, too many reasons to be sad, pissed, depressed, furious...and none of them I can do a thing about. Frankly, I don't have time to deal with them and if I don't get to pee alone, I'm not wasting my time being furious. I have these great kids who know how to push my buttons and drive me up a tree. I live in this great big 'ol house, that while it will have continuous issues, it's a labor of love. I have these neighbors that will help me when I need it. The only thing I don't have and obviously will need to stock up on in case of emergencies? SOUR MIX...

**...never mind, he's too short...**

...it's not that mysterious. Frankly, at times it's the thing of nightmares, but it's what we call our day to day. It starts earlier than I ever want, filled with drama, near fist fights, tantrums, NOISE, and at some point it ends, and I think, "...well, we survived (at times barely)...". And, come sun up, we get to do it all over again...

We reinstated "Everyone Helps Make the Meal" day again. It has been sort of chaotic in the last few months, and currently with a bum arm, I can use all the 'help' I can get. Oddly enough, "Everyone Cleans" day has never really gotten off the ground. If this cast has to stay on as long as I think, everyone, EVERYONE, will be adopting a new list of chores. While the kids enjoy helping with dinner, it is sort of reverse psychology- if they make it, and do not like it, they can't blame me. My Evil Genius degree is in the mail from the University of Phoenix as we speak...

This time, the 7th of the month snuck up on me. Maybe because we are healing through it, maybe because we've been away from home, maybe because we don't need to have a Shriner's Parade once a month anymore. In talking to the kids today, I realized that the latter may be true. They said that while it has been hard, it's getting easier every month. There are things they wish they had from their dad, but they know that the memory of what they want is going to have to get them through. As always, Nora is the most vocal about what she wants, and she's not afraid to tell me about it...plain and simple, she wants a dad. A couple of weeks ago, I saw her sizing someone up at a store. I asked what she was doing. She replied, "...never mind, he's too short..." While her openness is honorable, her honesty is frightening at times.

People in the last couple of weeks have asked me, how I do it? Not sure how to answer, I usually parlay that question into a joke involving the Betty Ford Clinic. The fact is, there is no real answer to that question. Has it always worked? No. Has it at times sucked? Yes. Has it made us all face our fears? Yes. Have we had to grow up faster than we wanted? Unfortunately, yes. Have we failed? At times, yes. Do we have a choice not to just do it? No....it's as if one question turns into a game of 20 questions....is it an animal, vegetable or mineral? We have a set list of 'goals' on our refrigerator, we made them together, and decided what we wanted to do....minus a request to shoot BB guns once a week. Sometimes we make our goals, sometimes we don't. Sometimes I leer at them, but then remind myself, what the hell else do I have to do tomorrow? Bottom line, we keep moving...I've trained myself to look beyond the clutter/dust/laundry...it can all be dealt with tomorrow. Now, that's not saying I'm not FLYING AROUND THIS HOUSE when I know someone is coming over!

I guess, through all this, at the end of the day there is no magic going on here...other than that of my seriously amazing kids. Their wisdom, their determination, their humor, their misguided (at times) line of thought...That's how I do it. That's how I keep going...plus, I have a million Betty Ford Clinic jokes...

**...this corn is so good (and then she pukes)...**

...box upon box, here and there...endless piles of stuff to put somewhere...sweat dripping off faces and dust in eyes. Repeated questions about where to put things....and the question uttered umpteen times, WHERE THE HELL DID WE GET ALL OF THIS STUFF? The feeling of starting over, new, exciting, endless possibilities...one year ago, the day we moved into this house.

Flash forward to the present. Atticus is EVERYWHERE, quickly, stealthy, relentlessly, and there isn't a corner, toilet, nook, or crevasse he hasn't explored. His siblings should be grateful that he had not been my first, otherwise they would have never been born. I see every day as part of his mountaineer training, hoping one day to be as legendary as Edmund Hillary on Everest. I'm to the point that if I happen to walk into a room and he is somehow swinging from the chandelier, I really won't be shocked, just bewildered what took him so long to figure it out.

Abe has taken to free climbing anything he possibly can...I'm sensing a pattern. He is constantly trying new and daring feats of strength and agility, climbing doorways and acting like he might be an extra from the Shanghai Circus. When he tires of that, he likes to 'wow' the ladies with some fabricated story of, "how he wrestled a bear to the ground on Highway 51(?). Not only does he have a scar, but one of the bears teeth to prove it..." I'm not making one word of that up. He tried to charm some girl in Taco Bell today with such absurdities, to which she looked at me like, "...could you get him to stop talking now?"

Nora, still on the quest for someone to "snuggle with" as she puts it (cute now, but I will be frowning on it in about 12 years), still is holding her ground with the self-appointed notion that there needs to be a man in this house. She mentioned to me the other day, she's "just looking for someone who can pick her up and throw her around, and they need to give good hugs". She also would like them to not eat green beans, as just the sight of a can of them the other day sent her into full on tears. The mere concept that they might be served for dinner sent her into negotiation mode. Putting away the tears long enough to tell me that she would eat corn, however we would have to shake on it to make it official. Quick question...WHAT? I shook on it, grateful not to have had to make a blood pact. At dinner, she took one bite, uttered something along the lines of, "...this corn is so good..." and then she gagged and puked. The multivitamin is going to have to do until she can get her reflexes together.

Oscar is growing like a weed, turning into a typical tween (yeah, he's 9, and I fully blame Disney Channel for that- well, and myself). He's interested in his hair...not deodorant, brushing his teeth, or looking clean, but his HAIR is a priority. He asked if we could buy hair spray the other day, I told him that first he'd have to shower daily. Secondly, he has his dad's hair- straight, thick, and STRAIGHT...it was going to take a lot more than hair spray to get it to do what he wants. He's looking forward to seeing his 'girlfriend' (I'm grateful she hasn't spent the summer texting me, as she got the hint I didn't want that relationship with her), and he mentioned to me today that he'd like to take piano lessons. So, I'm on the hunt for a student from the college. He also has had a dream about his dad, which I am so very grateful for. He, interestingly enough, didn't really remembered what the dream was about, just that he saw his dad and started crying tears of joy. Jason, keep it up, this one needs it more than any of us.

As for me, I average 4.67 minutes of adult TV during the day- I'm out voted. I mentally clean WAY MORE than I physically clean. I yearn to cook real food, that has real stuff in it, but I'm stunted for anyone to eat it. I long for conversation that doesn't involve the sub-plot of a superhero movie, Dora, or Elmo. I feel selfish at times for wanting an 'escape' from my day-to-day, as I feel like I should be thinking of the kids and taking them somewhere instead. I recognize that I am getting by, but could seriously be doing better...and that is going to take time. While I wish I could figure it all out right now and fix it, I can't. I guess the undertaking now is, I know what my heart wants/needs/misses. The goal is going to be finding it and making it all work...like I've got nothing else to worry about...

It's absurd how things can change in a year. And, while I wish the vibe one year later were the same, it just isn't. The other night, sleep deprived, after the kids were in bed, I walked through the house. I looked intently at every part of every room...trying to glean something from a year ago...some memory...something to make the crap sandwich of a day better. It seemed the harder I tried, the more I ended up thinking of the things I screwed up. The things I should have said. The moments I should have really, intensely treasured, instead of writing them off as ordinary. It seems that no matter how hard one tries, you can never go back in time and 'fix' things. So, a year later, I am in this beautiful house...terrified of all that it has to have done to it at some point...frightened of screwing it up...wishing I weren't alone in these endeavors. And even though at times I lose hope, I guess I'm still hopeful...

### ...when Apples to Apples Jr. lead to fisticuffs...

...it's crept in...it's a foreign noise at times...it's not every minute of the day, but when it's audible it's meaningful...it starts in the belly or at times it's just a chortle that sneaks up in your throat...it's laughter...and at times around here it is seemingly the best, only, least expensive, no need to drive the car to get it, medicine.

There are times in the last 9 months that we've needed it...yearned for it...willed it to happen, because really that is what we have always been about. For whatever reason, what once came so easy to us, eluded us. Maybe we caught ourselves, thinking we shouldn't be that happy, meanwhile wondering why we were so miserable. It seems that letting go, while at times is hard, finding laughter is even harder.

I feel like we had to trudge through this trail of ranging and raging emotions to find our 'new' center again...as if we had to realize that if we tried to find our 'happy' where we used to be, it wasn't how we remembered, only setting us back again. It was as if one day, we realized we are not only a little cynical about what has happened to us, seeing the other side has made us sort of different, new, whole again...because really we don't have a choice in the matter...

The thing is, I guess we have a choice, but it isn't one that anyone can suggest. It isn't as easy as just going to a movie, getting your nails done, getting a new toy. That is fleeting and in the end the hole you were attempting to fill, just seems more gaping...it's a mixture of hard work, patience (which, by the way NO ONE IN THIS HOUSE has), and trying to find the silver lining, almost until you want to puke!

Holding the puke at bay, we have settled
into a routine, which will soon change with
registration forms, checking homework and
sack lunches. We made it through the
summer, slightly unscathed, not hitting all of
our goals, and at times finding some well
needed laughter. To me, this is the time you
make your new year resolutions...this is the
time when you decide what you want to do
and need to do, so that you have something
to look forward to at the end of the week.
For me it's the chance to start over, scrap the
stupid things 'we'd really enjoy as a family'-
which never worked. Really, no one would
ever believe how volatile Apples to Apples
Jr. gets around this house-nothing short of a
fist fight every time...clearly, it won't make
our list of the 'new-year-to-do' list...

While I know that fall isn't here, I can feel
the changes starting to happen, and for
once...they don't terrify me. For once, I feel
like, "...you know, if things aren't perfect,
well that's pretty damned terrific that we
even know the difference". I feel like things,
while always chaotic, are starting to fall into
place. Make sense. And most importantly
look promising...and no, that's not the
cocktail talking. Even though my windows
need washing and I still set out the best

snack trays... It's the long sought after laughter that will hopefully keep coming back to visit...

Made in the USA
Lexington, KY
20 May 2015